inner healing for broken vessels

D1264557

INNER HEALING
FOR
BROKEN VESSELS

a domestic violence survival guide

LINDA H. HOLLIES

The Pilgrim Press
Cleveland

The Pilgrim Press, 700 Prospect Avenue, Cleveland, Ohio 44115-1100
thepilgrimpress.com
© 1992, 2006 Linda H. Hollies

Original edition © 1991 Woman to Woman Ministries, Inc. Publications
First published in 1992 by Upper Room Books, 1908 Grand Avenue,
Nashville, Tennessee 37212

"To Seleta" by Valerie Bridgeman Davis © 1985. Used by permission
of the author.

"The Broken Vessel" by Andraé Crouch. © 1968 by MANNA MUSIC, INC.,
25510 Stanford Ave., Suite 101, Valencia, CA 91355. International
Copyright secured. All rights reserved. Used by permission.

"A Personal Support Grid." Used by permission of Janice Eddy of the
Portsmouth Consulting Group, Kittery Pt., ME.

"I've Been Mixed Like Cornbread" by Raedorah C. Stewart ©1995 by
Raedorah C. Stewart © 1988. Used by permission of the author.

"I'm Crying Through" by Phenessa A. Gray. Used by permission of the author.

Biblical quotations are primarily from the New Revised Standard
Version of the Bible © 1989 by the Division of Christian Education of the
National Council of Churches of Christ in the United States of America,
and are used by permission.

All rights reserved. Published 2006

Printed in the United States of America on acid-free paper

10   09   08   07   06   5   4   3   2   1

Library of Congress Cataloging-in-Publication Data
Hollies, Linda H.
     Inner healing for broken vessels : a domestic violence survival guide /
Linda H. Hollies.
        p. cm.
     Includes bibliographical references.
     ISBN 0-8298-1714-X
     1. Women—Religious life.   2. Women—Conduct of life.   3. Spiritual
healing.   I. Title.

BV4527.H65   2005
248.8'43—dc22
                                                              2005029411

contents

acknowledgments

Pastoral care is a living art. It differs from most other types of care in that the person giving is also receiving. Pastoral care requires the ability to be vulnerable enough to allow others the opportunity to share your life experiences—including your pains, hurts, and failures. Mutual care and sharing is a good way to describe pastoral care in its fullest sense. There are many individuals who have contributed to my ability to provide "good" pastoral care.

I was brought into the world on the backs and in the womb of three strong African American women: my mother, Doretha Adams; Big Mama, Eunice Wade; and Grandmother, Lucinda Weston. They have all gone to be with God, but they left me a legacy of strong love and care for my family. These three women have taught me how to take a little and stretch it, how to love and to be loved, and how to rely on my faith in God. This faith has kept our family together. Also to my sisters, Jacqui, Riene, and Regina, and my brothers, James, Eddie, David, and Robert; I owe a debt of love.

My immediate family—husband, Charles; sons, Gregory and Grelon, now deceased; daughter, Grian; grandchildren, Giraurd, Gemal, and Symphony—have provided support in so many ways that words are not adequate to describe their love to me. These folk have been and are my "center" and allow me to come and to go, knowing that I have a place of refuge and security, which is essential for effective ministry. Especially I owe a debt I can never repay to Chuck, who is one of the strongest, most liberated men I have ever met.

My first role model of pastoral care was a sweet, gentle woman in the little church back home, Mother Louise Holloway. She, along with my pastor's wife, Evangelist Lula Smith, carried me after my mother gave me birth. Then God provided me with nurture through two instructors, who remain my friends, mentors, and sisters: seventh-grade English teacher Hortense House and college professor Della Burt-Bradley. Continuing comfort, care, collaboration, and confrontation have been given in various forms by good friends Barbara Baker VanBuren, Joyce Suggs Jordan, Elizabeth Clarke Brown, Darlene Sims Lee, Thelma Nunn Pryor, Madine Blakely, and Charmaine Hopkins. These women have been extended family through the years.

Attending Garrett-Evangelical Theological Seminary was one of the most rewarding experiences of my life. For three years it was the womb of learning, growing, and stretching that birthed my theological underpinnings. Here I met Rev. Jessica Ingram, who has listened, challenged, and "set with me" in ministry. Administrator Helen Fannings

took me to heart and "loved" me through the system! My
first models of professional, competent, and loving women in
ministry were Dr. Emma Justes and Dr. Emily Townes. Along
with these folk, peers Frankella Brandon, Brenda Heffner,
and Ida Easley met with me for early Monday morning
prayers at the lakeside and made the weeks bearable.

Seminary is more than relationships, it is learning. Dr.
Adolph Hanson, vice-president of Student Services, made
possible my education through his belief in my potential. I
praise God for this vessel of many blessings in my seminary
experiences. I had the fortunate opportunity to be exposed to
professors Richard Stegner, Robert Jewett, Lawrence
Murphy, Henry Young, and Edward Wimberly. They taught
me how to dig for the unsearchable riches in the scriptures.

I spent two years in Clinical Pastoral Education (CPE),
where theology is wed with clinical psychology. My supervisors, who dared to see more in me than I ever imagined, pulled
from me resources that have served me and others well. To
Beth Burbank, Dennis Kenny, JoClare Wilson, Joan Teems,
and Cynthia Smitko is due a great deal of gratitude for their
courage and willingness to "hang in there" with me until my
breakthrough and in my own journey toward inner healing.

And how do I begin to acknowledge Woman to Woman
Ministries, Inc. and the Richards Street United Methodist
Church, who have added to my pastoral care abilities? Each
entity has pulled, stretched, dilated, and increased my love for
ministry. Without either one of these resources I could not
have grown and become who I am today. Woman to Woman
Ministries, Inc. was born out of my own personal pain in 1985
as I reached out to other sisters who were undergoing their
own individual personal pain and wanted to be healed.
Through the encouragement of Daisy Thomas-Quinney,
Beverly Garvin, Deborah Tate, Eleanor Miller, Terrell Cistrunk,

Elizabeth Garcia, Joyce E. Wallace, Samatha Kendell, Harlene Harden, Freddie Ammons, and others like them, my life has become enriched. They have worked, sacrificed, and carried the load when I could not.

The list of those who have contributed to the becoming of this particular manuscript is endless, for it encompasses all those who have touched my life, entered into my space, and allowed me to enter theirs in return.

This book is gratefully dedicated to Charles, Greg, Grelon, Grian, Giraurd, Gemal, and Symphony, my family; to Woman to Woman Ministries, Inc., and every sister who plays a part in it; to every woman who has dared to share her life with me, to grace me with the gift of herself; to those who have worked diligently to pull together workshops, seminars, retreats, Women's Days, support groups, and other avenues whereby I could both minister and be ministered to in return; and to every pastor who opened doors and allowed me entrance to give nurture, guidance, and sustenance to women, while I learned so much about myself.

I give God thanks for you, the reader, who will sit with me, journey with me, and take off on your own process toward inner healing and wholeness. You are each in my prayers, for as we grow, change, and evolve, we touch others; and the world is continually being made a better place for all of us. I close by simply expressing thanks to God for the grand privilege of being a vessel, broken in my youth, and yet glued in so many places by so many loving persons. To God be the glory for each one of you. May the shalom of our God be yours!

p r e f a c e

One day I walked into a curio shop and was immediately attracted to a beautiful gold vase. I just knew it was too expensive, but the beauty was startling. As I oohed and ahhed, I was afraid to pick it up and inquire about its price. The salesperson approached me and asked if I was interested in such a rare find. Hesitatingly, I confessed my inability to pay for such an article. The salesperson said, "It's on sale." As she picked up the fragile looking artifact and handed it to me, she told me to look at its interior. Inside was a complexity of lines and scratches. They told a different story than the exterior beauty. They told of the difficulty the designer had while trying to complete this vase.

Immediately the title of this book, *Inner Healing for Broken Vessels,* came to mind. That vase tells the story of so many of us, who look good and together on the outside but have wounded interiors. There are designer dresses, shoes, accessories, and perfumes to cover the broken hearts and crushed spirits of women. Executive jobs and prestigious positions enfold many women who have wounds inside that none of us ever see.

The ugly insides reduced the price of this vase until it now sits in my home. Our wounds have given us value because God can now use us in the healing of others. May this book serve as a source of your inner healing.

introduction

THE CIRCLE OF HEALING

The year was 1991. Our daughter, Grian, had come from her first year of college, pregnant! I was serving a huge church with less than one hundred people on the rolls. The bills were large, and the offerings were not large enough. The black people in the neighborhoods were skeptical of us, but the black gang members stood on our church parking lot and across the street at the corner store and hustled drugs. It was my very first church to pastor. I was struggling to just keep my head above water. I felt so engulfed by sorrow, so bereft of love, and I was so afraid of failing!

Both of my parents had died. Now my last grandmother was crossing to the other side of eternity, in a nursing home, wrestling with Alzheimer's. I seemed to be overwhelmed all the time. My tears were always present. My dreams were of me drowning in murky, green, nasty-looking waters. I wanted to run away. I wanted some place of escape. I wanted to put my head down in the sand. But I was the spiritual leader of a congregation. I was supposed to have answers for others.

How could I make it through this season of loss? What were the lessons that I was to learn from my pain? Who were the people that I could turn to for examples of overcoming all the mess? Of course, as a preacher with seminary experience, I began to go backwards in my thinking. I began to reflect upon how I had made it through other troubling times. And I began to write in order to remember a time of feeling joy, a time of feeling whole and a time of being loved. The results are within the pages of this book, *Inner Healing For Broken Vessels*

What I discovered was that most of us have a warped sense of the word "love." This twisted, messed-up, and often dirty concept of a misused and misunderstood word often stems from some pain that we have experienced in our childhood. As a preteen, I had been raped by my father in the name of "love." This surely messed up my mind! Love is not to cause hurt. Love is not to be kept secret. Love is not to make us feel ashamed. But in the name of "love," incest was committed. The shame took on a life of its own as I sought the best ways that I could find to cover it, mask it, and keep others from knowing my secret.

This confusion and paranoia and the painful pit in the bottom of my stomach caused me to grow up and to behave in some strange ways seeking "love." Lenard Sweet, in his book *The Jesus Prescription for a Healthy Life*, painted my portrait and I want to share those (my) symptoms with you.

1) I stayed busy all the time, doing for others, but seldom took "me time." 2) I attempted to please everyone else so that I could feel loved. 3) I did most things by myself, because I could not trust others. 4) I refused to ask anyone for help because it made me feel too vulnerable. 5) I visited all the serious food buffets in town, across town, and out of town. 6) I never exercised and my weight kept creeping up. 7) I rarely laughed and never played games. Life was no fun! 8) I took myself extremely seriously and tried never to fail. 9) I tried diligently to be in control of all situations, by any means necessary! 10) I refused to join any group where hard questions were asked and I had to be accountable to others. I continue to appreciate Dr. Sweets' research, which helped me to see myself clearly.

Yet I felt as if I were seeking for love. In reality, I was stressed out to the max, running on empty most of the time, and at the point of self-destruction. I had no idea of what love was, neither how to get it or how to receive it. For I had to learn that love is a competition in both giving and receiving! Love is not selfish, seeking only to satisfy its own lust. Love is not pain, violating you and making you ashamed. Love is not secret keeping. And love is not violent, destructive, or abusive. Love is not lust. Love is not a booty call. Love is not disrespect. Love is not a sugar daddy or a stupid, walk-all-over-me woman!

Love is mutual. Love is safe. Love provides. Love respects. Love protects. Love is shared. Love is caring, comforting, collaborating, clarifying, and even confronting in truth. And, love celebrates in community. For we have to remember and to always keep in mind that, first and foremost, God is love! It's from God's love that the base of our human love grows. God cares for us. God cares about us. God so loved that God gave Jesus to die for us so that we might have a relationship again. Love is about selflessness and self-giving.

In America, we have overused and misused the word "love." We say that we "love" chocolate. We claim that we "love" our new car. We "love" the outfit that someone has on. Chocolate is not all that good for us, and we eat it up too fast, not actually enjoying it. Cars rust, break down, and won't start when it gets too cold. And awesome outfits don't fit our shapes, personalities, and pocketbooks forever either! So there goes the word "love."

If we are going to get to the bottom of our dilemma with this powerful word, we need to look at its several meanings. There is "eros" love, a Greek word meaning sexual (erotic) desire. This type of love is based on the ego of the lover. The person desired becomes an object to reflect who the lover feels that he or she is. Ego love tends to dominate. Ego love will smother. Ego love will even hurt its object in order to have its way. Be careful of love based on someone's ego. It might be the "I've got to have you" syndrome that fades after sex. All eros love is based on personal ego.

Then there is "familia" love or family love. There are kinfolks whom we have to accept, relate to, and stay in touch with—even as crazy as they are. None of us is an island. None of us is the result of an immaculate conception where we don't have that group of folks that we'd like to walk away from and not have to deal with at some point in time. But family is as family does. We didn't choose our family. Hopefully, we come out better when choosing the person we decide to share our sacred space and, ultimately, our lives with for the long run. But beware: until we deal with our childhood stuff, too many of us women select men who are as messed up as "dear old dad." And every dad, regardless of how good, how loving, and how handsome, has issues.

We can stop the lie that we had perfect parents. I have issues. You have issues. All of God's children have issues! That means all of us are messed up and, therefore, we have to come to the word, "agape," which means the unconditional love of God. This unconditional love accepts us, warts and all. An unconditional love realizes that there is no perfection in any human being! We are all in process of becoming day by day. Unconditional love seeks to allow others the room to grow, the ability to change and to further develop as we age, wise up, and mature. An unconditional love can wait until the proper time for sex and all of its complications. An unconditional love is a competition in giving to and receiving from the other. Agape love allows me to follow Jesus' command to love my neighbor, as I love myself.

In order to love my neighbor as I love myself, I am not to love my neighbor better than I love myself. I am not to love my neighbor less than I love myself. My priority is to love the God who created me, and then to love the creatures whom God has made like me! I am to love my neighbor, as I love myself. The key word is "as." "As" implies that I have self-love, self-respect, and self-esteem going for me first! Because, if I cannot love me, there is no possible way that I can love another! Without self-love, I am stressed and seeking for love outside of me. Then, most times, the love I am seeking will be found in all the wrong places!

Stress, anxiety, and frustration will cause us to do crazy, insane, and unsafe stuff in the name of love. As women, we have some good reasons. First and foremost is our socialization process. We can pretend that the women in the Middle East and Far East have it bad, but if we really tell the truth, most of us are not as far along to self-actualization as we need to be either. We have been socialized to be "nice little girls." We are socialized to be "seen and not heard." We are socialized to cater to the men around us. We are socialized to take care of others first and to put ourselves last. Remember that old slogan about JOY being Jesus, others and finally yourself? It's a lie! We are socialized to believe that women can't get along and can't trust each other. And we have bought what we were sold.

So women tend to isolate from one another. We tend to look for men to validate our personhood. We tend to shy away from the sisterhood, for who wants to be bothered with a group of women who can't stand each other and don't know too much in the first place? Therefore, many of us take on multiple roles to stay busy and to not take the time to deal with our personal issues. We refuse to learn how to "just say no!" We will wear ourselves out trying to do the impossible. It's time to pull off and to cut up our Superwoman capes and destroy them!

Most women have difficulty expressing anger, for they don't want to be called the "b" word! We have been socialized never to show our anger. However, anger is a valid emotion that is healthy when we learn how to deal with it nonaggressively. There are some soft sounding statements that can address our highest level of "pissivity" without sounding rough. "I resent that." "I don't like that." "I refuse to allow you to say that to me again." "I won't stand for this type treatment again." Practice saying them now, in your soft tone. These sentences allow you to keep your power and refrain from going off like a "b"! Yet, using these power sentences permits us to correctly inform folks, even supervisors and significant others, of our anger with civility and proper language.

Holding our anger inward will kill us. If we hold it too long, we just might kill someone else! For hidden anger becomes rage that is uncontrollable at it's zenith.

Anger is a good thing when we recognize that it's only the other side of our hand. One side is anger and the other side is hurt. We cannot control our hurt, and we lie to ourselves to believe that we can control our anger by hiding it away. It will erupt if not dealt with in time. When we speak our anger and share our anger we can make giant changes in life. Every major gain in the world has been accomplished because some angry people got together and demanded change from the way things had been before. Get your anger outside of you. Look at it. Then, decide if it needs to be shared and with whom.

Stress, anxiety, and frustration can be caused by our "do it all" syndromes. This is the pattern that we have too often seen in our mothers, who learned it from their mothers, who learned it from their mothers, who might have learned it from a slave master. This leads to the issue of our doing it all and trying to do it perfectly instead of learning lessons from doing our best and failing forward. Failure is really a teacher, an instructor. Failure is not ever fatal unless we choose to stop growing, stop learning, and stop loving our ability to learn new lessons from life.

Another big issue of stress for most of us is the need for others to approve us and our efforts. It's a human trait to want affirmation. But when we "need" affirmation in order to survive, it becomes an enemy of our health. There comes a time in our lives when we have to learn how to stretch our own arms, use our own hands, and pat ourselves on the back for a job well done! When we have given our best and done all that we can, it's all that life requires until the next time. The next time we can use the lessons that we have learned in order to go a different way, try other options, and seek alternative methods. Great inventions come only as the result of our trying to make better something that has failed.

I wish that I could declare to you that fifteen years
after writing this book I've learned all my lessons and was
at the top of my game. It would be a lie. For as far as I've
moved, I continue to deal with sexual harassment, racism,
and classism. Dealing with being a triple "minority" causes
great stress. So I learned early on the imposter phenomenon,
using a mask to be who "they" need me to be. It requires
much inner healing as I go back, time and time again, to the
Source of my being for more healing balm. Life is continually difficult. The journey to my own inner healing is a
tough road. The road is long, curving, and has winding
ways and dips, along with dangerous curves that show up
without notice. The journey is not impossible. This is my
good news to you.

After recognizing my wounds, I found sisters who allowed me to admit how I had been working with false and
incomplete information. A healing circle of women have been
there for me to be real, open, honest, and vulnerable as I
cried out loud, "I'm just a broken vessel. I've been fooled
with education, jobs, and positions. But I want to wake up. I
want to grow. I want to change." And my healing circle of
sisters has held and continues to hold my feet to the fire.

When we can share our new reality and new decision
with those who have proved trustworthy and true, we grow.
This group becomes an accountability group, a discipleship
group, a healing circle, a church group or a book club where
we can talk and get feedback and honest clarity. It's in groups
of sisterly community that others can lovingly confront us
and help us to clarify our issues from our fairy tales and fantasies. When the time came to deal with my incest issues, I
had to have someone say to me that it was alright to be
angry! That it was alright to cry! For my anger had scared me
and I'd been socialized to believe that tears were signs of

anger. Thank God for the women who confronted me and helped me to grow and to change.

The fifth step of inner healing is a tricky one—the step of reconciliation. This is the time for our letting go of our need for revenge against the one who has hurt us, abused us, and violated us. Reconciliation is not a time of going back into a painful, harmful relationship. Reconciliation is not the return to those who have not asked for our forgiveness or been willing to make amends. Rather, reconciliation comes when I'm willing to lay down my tools of war. It happens when I withdraw my energies for repayment from the one who hurt me in the first place. Reconciliation is when I can honestly and wholeheartedly give that person over into God's hand for vengeance.

My reconciliation did not come with eye-to-eye contact with my father. Reconciliation for us took place way after he was dead and buried. I wrote him a long letter and took it to the cemetery and read it aloud and then tore the letter up to allow it to fly into the four winds. I do not ever expect God to wipe the memories of my pain away. I cannot simply forgive and forget. It's not that easy. But I did forgive. I did forego my need to see my father pay for the sin he committed against me. I became reconciled to the fact that he must face God in the long run.

It continues to be my personal decision to be different, to grow, to change, and to stop being stuck in yesterday's pain. The sixth step of my Inner Healing has become an optimistic and realistic view of my life. I give focused attention to me and to the priorities of my life. I have purpose. I have destiny. I have a ministry to women. I make lists of my goals and I check them often. I have learned how to say no. I have learned how to delegate tasks, to ask for help, and to make sure that I don't try to do everything by myself. I have chosen to be open to learning new things, meeting new people, and discovering new ways to increase my personal effectiveness. This is my choice. These are my options. I choose to move with life's flow and not be stuck without quality self-love operating within me!

My day starts with journaling, scripture reading according to the lectionary (a devotional book works for me), and then I spend time in prayer. I try to have lunch with a motivating girlfriend a least once a week. I call inspiring folks to drop into WomanSpace for tea. I take time off to go and visit the uplifting, doing something, ongoing, forward-thinking women who have offices on the floor with me. And I keep inspirational music going during my day. Choosing life means for me that about ten o'clock at night I take my phone off the hook. I have given away all of that day's supply. It's time for me to be replenished. The television is off. After Giraurd goes to bed and Mista Chuck watches the news and argues with the television, I get into bed and chill. This hour is my unwinding time. I read magazines, flip through the pretty scenes, learn new things, consider new ideas, and read good fiction.

On a daily basis I choose life and love! My love life begins with me! I choose a healthy, balanced lifestyle. I work and I have fun. I continue my education by reading, attending college and seminary classes, and teaching at both WomanSpace and at the local extension of the University of Phoenix that keeps me in contact with moving-ahead adults.

I go to worship and enjoy movies, theater, and good books. I spend time with my family, especially Mista Chuck and Giraurd, who is now fifteen and a sophomore in high school. He is tall, dark, dimpled, good-looking, and a joy to have in our lives! I eat well and Lady Duchess, my dog, keeps me walking. I choose to purchase quality walking shoes. For I like good food and I will move this body and work off calories. I do not eat all that I want for I want to live and to be my very best. I drink plenty of water, for our bodies are 70 percent water and need to be hydrated. Taking care of me, because my body is God's temple, has become essential.

My sister readers, it's been a busy fifteen years and it's been a full fifteen years. My son Grelon Renard has died from the complications of diabetes. Both myself and Greg have diabetes also. Grelon's death, although painful, was a teaching tool about choosing life. Grian has continued to make me choose life by going in and out of prisons due to her choices. She is a beautiful young woman who has another ten-year-old son, Gemal, and a seven-year-old daughter, Symphony. Grian will be released soon, and, I'm going to include one of her poems as I ask you to continue to hold her and my grandchildren in your prayers. Mista Chuck has finally retired and gone back to work again. He works, plants a garden, and fixes things around our house and those of other friends to keep himself active and energized. He's my best friend and I'm so thankful for our marriage. Greg works in Southfield for a major phone service supplier and treats me like a queen mother! When money got tight for us, he started to send his mom a monthly allowance for hair and nails! To say that I love him would be an understatement.

I'm a living witness that we can find love in the right places. We can define love and know that love's order is to love God first, me second, and all others after that. We can overcome our former delusions regarding love. We can set realistic goals. We can realize that we are not God, so perfection is not expected of us. We will give our best. We will recognize our limitations and allow for mistakes; acknowledge our mistakes——admit our mistakes and learn the lessons of our mistakes. We will learn how to pace ourselves. When I work for an hour, my knees demand that I take a twelve-to-fifteen-minute stretch break! I light candles at my computer so that the smoke can talk to God for me. I make phone calls all across the country to keep in touch with my sister-friends. I will read and even forward good e-mail jokes. And I try to play soft, wordless, elevator music so that my heart rate slows down and I can feel that calm returning to my center in the midst of a busy day. All work and no play will make anyone of us dull and listless women!

Learn to give back to your community by reading to children or mentoring a little sister. We did not make it alone. Neither can they. Read books for fun. Leaf through magazines. Watch funny videos for laughter's sake. Zone out and daydream. Nap. Write down ten things that have brought you joy in the past, and then relive those moments with a friend. Schedule time to do at least two of these things again soon.

I've gone through the seven steps to inner healing many, many times and I've discovered that life is not all bad! Sadness comes, but it does not stay. Love is not just a word, it's a reality that we need to encounter. The best love begins as we learn to heal our childhood wounds and make friends with the little girl who lives inside. She's been lonely and she's been afraid. Now, since you are willing to choose to grow up, you can reassure her that indeed, "everything will be alright!" For if God has brought the time of healing to you, trust God to see you through it. Inner healing belongs to the people of God. Let your healing process begin. There is no better time than now! There is no better place than within a healing circle of sisters and friends. I pray God's divine benediction upon us all as you read Grian's growing poem and grow too!

Who Am I?

I am the much loved daughter of Linda, Charles, and
    James. I am the result of a blended family.
I am the mother of Girarud, Gemal, and Symphony.
I am a regal descendant of Queen Nzinga.
I am a daughter of the Earth.
I am sun, moon, stars, water, and air.
I am as open as the Grand Canyon—to the prickling realities
    and innumerable possibilities the world has to offer.
I am Spirit.
I am the awe and beauty of procreation.
I am fertile—not just in childbearing—
but in ideas, creativity, and the unlimited bountifulness
    of the universe.
I am evolution—forever changing and progressing forward
    toward the ultimate me.
I am revolution—fighting to be who I am against your
    standards.
My illusions of grandeur had me pretend to be Robin Hood,
    in the hood.
My defiance volunteered me to be Kizzie for the state,
identified by 6 digits behind fences and wire.
The chains do not imprison me.
I am free,
free to tell my story, free to morph into my rightful place
    of greatness.
I am a colored girl that considered life.
I am outside your box.
I have a voice. I will be heard.
I am music—I am jazz riffs floating in the wind.
I am the pulsing bass line of hip-hop.
I am the operatic high C that can shatter glass.
I am the translator between human and trees;

the toke and release of sweet citronella smoke is
my conversation with nature.
I am the embodiment of love.
I am a faithful concubine whose skin has been kissed
     by the sun.
I am a statuesque High Priestess with full hips,
voluptuous curves, and eyes that glimmer like
diamonds.
I am hope. I am peace. I am a survivor.
I am more than a conqueror.
You cannot define me.
I am the master of my destiny.
I am worthy of honor.
I am every woman.
I am the Truth.
I am Grian Eunyke.

—Grian E. Hollies Terry Anthony,
Huron Valley Correctional Center for Women,
Ypsilanti, Michigan

1

s t e p   o n e

RECOGNITION

The conference for women had ended and five of the executives sat in a hotel suite eating pizza and laughing over some particulars of this intense weekend. Pajamas and fun were the order of the night as we evaluated speakers, workshops, and participants. As is the pattern for any gathering of women, talking turned to personal issues. Although we represented four different denominational groups, our stories ran along parallel lines. As we shared personal and often painful matters, Terry obviously wanted to make a joke of her own inner struggles. Finally, she was asked the very pointed question, "What is your laughter attempting to cover?"

The pause was pregnant as we awaited her response. As she wrestled to articulate years of hurt, the tears began and she slid to a sitting position on the floor. One of the women knelt beside her and cradled her head to her bosom and began to rock this grown woman. Five powerful women cried together in the quiet of a raging storm. A time of recognition had arrived. A new beginning was being born. We were the midwives to Terry's claim that the constant and consistent hurt held her fast, denying her authentic selfhood and her inner core of true existence. The tears spoke volumes of an emptiness that words could not describe.

THE SHARED REALITIES OF WOMEN

Women have an inner connection that needs no articulation. Our shared realities speak of our union of tradition and of crisis. Sorrow is our foremother. Suffering and striving are our aunts. Begin-all-over-again is our maternal grandmother. And our name is Wait! Women have a history of living under whips, lashes, and men's feet. We have sometimes been confined within even loving walls, called bondage. Our feet tell the story of many travels.

Through the exodus in the wilderness we have come. We have waited in the lush forests of Ethiopia, the tropical wilds of Kenya, and in the palaces of Egypt. We have waited in the cotton fields, the rice paddies, and the migrant fields. Often we have waited in the big houses that have not been our homes. We have been waiting for others to recognize our worth and to give us our due. Like Terry, many of us laugh to keep from crying. But the recognition of our own personal, authentic existence comes to each of us.

TERRY'S STORY

Terry is an executive with a major corporation. She has been recognized as a major force by her company and was given the highest award ever given to a nonengineer. She drives a luxury car and carries two gold cards. She is a wife and mother of three. And yet, she was not fulfilled. To the outside world she looked like a success, but on that night of the pizza party, the interior hurts were revealed.

Born into a family of six children to a young, unmarried woman, Terry can distinctly remember the pain of never being recognized by the man who was her biological father. She lived in the same small town, where she saw him often, but no relationship was ever established. Poverty was a way of life. Stealing food and coal were survival methods employed by both brothers and sisters. Not having decent housing or clothes were other endured pains. School became her escape. Here Terry could be recognized for her outstanding contributions. Books gave her insights into a world that was waiting. She was awarded a scholarship to college. This seemed to be the way out.

People who know misfortune can recognize that there are never "happily-ever-after" endings to such stories. After living on a treadmill of misery and going nowhere immediately, Terry's young mother, who had never really lived, died. How could Terry go merrily off to college while her brothers and sisters remained locked in poverty? She decided to forego further education in order to make money for her family. After graduation, Terry married her high school sweetheart, boarded a bus, and traveled from her southern roots to the North. Factories and steel mills were booming in the sixties, and immediately both husband and wife were employed. A son entered the picture, but sending money back home was a continued priority. Her sisters and brothers left the home site to migrate north, and although she was not the oldest child, Terry became the family matriarch. Every endeavor was dedicated to doing what her mother could not do—saving her children from a history of poverty and making a name for her family. Even today, the family business is named after the young mother who died so early and so empty. But when could Terry seek her own destiny and pursue her own dreams? When would her family applaud her efforts, say thanks, and push her to move ahead for her own survival?

VASHTI'S STORY: PERSONAL RECOGNITION

Each of us, as women, has been given basic rights and privileges by God. We are bequeathed the powers of creativity and birth, mandated to bring forth new images, new beings, and new things. For although we are made a little lower than angels (Heb. 2:7), we are God's daughters. And as daughters of the reigning Sovereign of this world, we are the head and not the tail. We are the apple of God's eye. Our names are engraved in God's hand where we can never be forgotten nor assigned a second-class status. As daughters of God we long for unity, wholeness, and recognition that nothing can repress or deny.

The first chapter of the Book of Esther outlines the details of a suppressed woman, Vashti. The story is told of the king who had been partying with his cabinet members for six months, taking stock of the resources he had amassed. He paraded his objects before the assembly. On the last day of the party, all had been given a different styled goblet and invited to drink their fill of alcoholic beverage to celebrate the success and great fortune of the king. It was a party of lust-filled men ruled by drink. The king decided that there was one more "object" that he needed to show off to his subjects. He sent seven men to bring him the queen, Vashti.

Now, we must understand that he was not calling the queen to have her address her loyal subjects. She was not sent for in order to allow her to be seen as his equal, co-monarch. No, she was "fetched" in order that the men in the kingdom could view her as an object, a thing that the king owned, a possession—truly a beautiful thing, but a thing nevertheless. The king sent seven eunuchs into her courts to escort her to his palace. While she was busy entertaining their wives, her guests, these men entered her quarters and declared that they had been told to bring her to the king. On this day, she said "No!"

History proves that Vashti had been queen for a long time. She was accustomed to her husband's behavior. She had been trained in how to please the monarch and groomed for over a year before becoming queen. She made it her business to know what he liked and what he disliked. For years she had lived her life at his command and for his pleasure. But today, she experienced personal recognition.

Scripture does not detail exactly what she experienced, but each one of us has our own story to tell of that particular day when something switched on, and we changed and became different inside. For it was on that day that we became free women. We follow the same routine, day after day, until one day we awaken and know that an interior change has occurred. Something inside is different and our response on that day will not be the same. You know that the time for change has come. Whatever happened yesterday will not be repeated today, "No, not today!" On this day, Vashti awakened with a different mindset, a different set of values. On this day she thought differently about herself. Her opinion of herself as a free woman surfaced, and her realities and priorities were not the same.

We have heard and reheard the story of Esther, without paying much attention to this woman, Vashti, who actually changed the course of history and allowed Esther her role. The Book of Ecclesiastes, chapter 3, reminds us that there is a time for every purpose under the heavens; the timing of the life of this, our sister, was no accident. Before any major change is enacted, there is always a cycle of actions and re-actions. Nothing just happens. There is always cause, and then effect. Vashti was in God's timing cycle. Without her significant action on that particular day, there never would have been an Esther on the scene to save the Jewish nation.

This day was a day of recognition for Vashti. "Queen Vashti refused to come" says the scripture. The scripture goes on to say that even the men knew the significance of her ac-tions. The men recognized that if women in the kingdom knew of their inner authority, the days of subservience would be over. If women took the time to go within and tap into their pool of inner strength and direction, what a different world we would have. For too long, many of us have abdicated our God-given rights and responsibilities to create and to build. We have buried our dreams and aspirations to follow another's path. But personal recognition will not be denied forever.

Vashti paid a high price for her recognition of her self-hood. She was forced to surrender her royal throne. Her household allowance and maid service were forfeited. The privilege of wearing the royal designer gowns was gone. The empty title of queen was even withdrawn. Her name was wiped from the pages of history, never to be mentioned again.

We must be willing to pay the price. For some of us it means that our secure positions, our empty titles, and our meaningless existences must be put on the line for our sakes and for our daughters and sisters who will come after us. Esther could only walk into the king's chambers unbidden because, one day, Vashti had refused to come.

CHOOSING FREEDOM

Giving up security is difficult. Terry was secure in her role as matriarch. When money, influence, and positions were needed, you could count on Terry. What would her new role in the family look like? The time of transition between what we have been and what our new role will be is a difficult period. We know the past, as painful as it has been. Not knowing the future is scary. And still, the time comes in our lives when we must decide, like Vashti, what actions we will take. And this is the time when we must stand up, prepared to move out, to move up, and to move on without help from anyone but the Creator God. For Vashti had to act without collaboration.

Most of the great achievers of our history had no committee from whom to seek advice, no support groups for comfort and consolation. But when freedom of the mind arrives, one is forced to act. African theologian Alan Bosak has said that the greatest gift we can give to those who would oppress us is our mind. For when your mind is shackled, no amount of legislation is going to cause you to move. But no one can control your mind without your willing assistance. Recognition forces us to acknowledge that freedom is a choice for us to consider.

BIRTHING A NEW LIFE OF WHOLENESS

In answer to the question, "Terry, what is your laughter an attempt to cover?" came the recognition that it was time for a change. On that night freedom came to Terry. Freedom from the chains of her past. Freedom for moving into a new future designed for her to achieve abundant life. She acknowledged her willingness to let the past dictate her choice to be the victim for her family. For although she gave much, she received little in return, not even appreciation. She recognized how few of her life's ambitions had been fulfilled and how little she thought of her own needs and desires. Recognition brought an awareness of how she sought "mothers" who would give her affirmation and allow her to "do for them" as she wanted to do for her dead mother. She remained in empty relationships with men for the affiliation she never received from her biological father. And she admitted that she covered her hurts with laughter.

A pizza party turned into a birthing session as Terry recognized that there was an emotional wound causing a vast emptiness in her life. She was tired of being viewed as the great Earth Mother to her family, an object of use and not a woman with needs, ambitions, and emotions.

Terry has grown since that pizza party. Some very definite changes have occurred in her life, all for the better. She has set some personal goals and has begun to take the steps to actualize them. She has cut the cords to some damaging relationships and enlarged her field of contacts with others. She began to make some personal demands for her life and was challenged by the powers that existed. This was to be expected. But the force of personal freedom and creative expression is blossoming within her life. She has not done anything drastic—no change of denomination, no divorce—but the inner reality has prompted a maturity in responding to and planning for her own abundant living.

She took a giant step into the unknown territory of change and has found the path to inner healing, for recognition is the acknowledgment of the sin of self-denial of our personhood, our womanhood, and our authentic self.

GROWTH EXPERIENCES

1. Have you allowed your roles in life to suppress and deny your authentic existence?

2. Have others defined your reactions to life and confined you to a position that is limited and restrictive?

3. If you, like Terry and Vashti, know that a new reality is seeking you, perhaps a listing of the many roles you fulfill might be helpful. For example, wife, mother, friend, sister, daughter, aunt, employee, employer, lover, significant other, church woman, club woman.

4. Which ones did you willingly take on?

5. Which ones do you choose today?

6. If any significant role were removed from your life, would you yet have an identity?

7. Can you define yourself apart from your roles?

8. What makes you authentic?

9. Read the passage about Vashti and answer the question "What do I need to refuse to do?"

2

step two

ADMISSION

The shrill ring of the telephone awakened me, and as I struggled to summon a coherent "hello," the cry, "Linda, I'm losing it!" jarred me into full wakefulness. Zinnia had been wrestling with the pain of a forthcoming divorce action for months. She was involved in professional counseling with a psychiatrist who had prescribed antidepressants and recommended that she participate in our woman's support group. She was not an hysterical woman, but one who appeared to have it all together. But now she was on the edge, a vessel ready to admit her need for inner healing.

ZINNIA'S STORY

Zinnia is a nursery school administrator. She is married and has a young son. She is in an interracial marriage, which had caused a wide breach in her family of origin. Her mother had died several years earlier, while her dad remained at the family home. She has several brothers and sisters, but is close to none of them. A very private, almost reclusive woman, Zinnia has few friends with whom to share her life. A member of our congregation, she slips into a rear pew and leaves immediately after worship. The many rejections of her life have caused her to think and feel that she is unworthy of love. The early years found Zinnia growing up in a very dysfunctional family. Her mother was the family tyrant, always screaming abusive and negative phrases and using illness to gain sympathy. This might well have been her mother's defense, since her husband (Zinnia's father) was a closet alcoholic.

THE LOST CHILD

In this type of family each person takes on a role in order to maintain harmony. The harm of these roles always emerges in adult life. Zinnia was the "lost child" of her family. The characteristics of the lost child are being shy, distant, withdrawn, aloof, hidden, and "invisible." Being a lost child afforded her the privilege of hiding from the family fights and confusion. However, being a lost child never taught her to fight for herself.

The lost child grows up to become the "Bo-Peep" woman. (Bo-Peep lost her sheep and didn't know where to find them!) In adulthood, these women often become almost antisocial and have suicidal tendencies. Rumbling within them are feelings, overwhelming feelings, of loneliness, rejection, inadequacy, fear, hurt, and anger, which they have not learned to recognize, sort out, and deal with. But eventually the day arrives when they voice the feelings, "I'm losing it!"

Dysfunctional families might appear unusual to those of us standing on the outside, but the family participants think that their family is the norm. The daily confusion and chaos is what they are accustomed to dealing with and living in, so they seek to find an extension of this family type in their marriages. Zinnia found a combination of both of her parents in her husband. He was a large man, filled with anger and self-hate, who vented his frustrations on her. This man was the person she was trying to leave after seven years. He had been without a job for two years, and Zinnia had been supporting the family, but not to his satisfaction. In the midst of the storm, an unplanned pregnancy developed.

After three months of emotional upheaval, severe stress, and general unhappiness, Zinnia miscarried. The day after, while she was still in the hospital, her husband announced that he was leaving her for another woman who "understood" him. Total rejection! As I stood by her hospital bed, trying to find the words to comfort this woman who had just lost a baby and had now been kicked in the stomach again, I thought of the story of Hagar in the scriptures. For like Zinnia, Hagar had been mistreated by a sister and then rejected by the primary male in her life. Hagar's healing came while she too wrestled in a desert place.

HAGAR: A WOMAN REJECTED

The story of this rejected woman comes in the Book of Genesis, chapters 16 and 21. A servant woman with no prestige, no power or influence, Hagar had been given to Sarai, the wife of wealthy Abraham, as a maid. When Sarai was not able to give her husband a son, she told him to have sex with Hagar, as any child she would bear "belonged" to him.

Hagar gave birth to a son, Ishmael. Her sense of self-importance caused by her ability to bear a son allowed her to look with disdain upon Sarai. This self-important attitude caused friction between the two women. Sarai had Abraham banish both Hagar and Ishmael on two separate occasions. The second time was after Sarai had given birth to her own son, Isaac. She was afraid that the older boy might become a usurper to the younger one's inheritance.

As Hagar struggled through the desert, where her water supply had run dry, she separated herself a bit from her son—in order not to watch him die from thirst. The angel of God came and asked, "What troubles you, Hagar? Fear not." I'm almost positive that this woman of many years ago sounded like Zinnia on the telephone: "I'm losing it!" It was an admission of inner pain, the hurts built over the years. To be mistreated by a sister is one thing, but to be rejected by this male with whom she created a son was simply too much to bear. This was not the time for being strong. This was not the time for denial of the pain. Hagar admitted to herself that the wound of constant and continual rejection had much power over her life and affected her every action and reaction in life. This act of admission and confession was her first step to inner healing.

The angel gave her the follow-up plan: "Fear not." This sounds like a giant step, and it is, but there is much wisdom in this phrase. Fear robs us of the ability to think and plan rationally. Fear dissipates our energies, robs us of our critical thinking skills, and causes us to waste precious time feeling sorry for ourselves. Fear is the largest impediment to our doing things differently and forces us to remain deadlocked in unfulfilling habits and patterns of relating. It is not easy to rid ourselves of fears, but it is possible if we do it a step at a time.

REACHING OUT FOR HELP

Zinnia's first step in ridding herself of her fear was to seek spiritual counsel. Too many ministers have not been trained in the art of pastoral counseling and dispense harmful information. The Christian church has been one of the biggest enslavers of women by quoting to them scriptures that maintain the status quo. The church through the years has been tied to the traditional norms and expectations of our society, which have often been in favor of men's rights over women's rights. Many male pastors come to the ministry never having worked through their own psychological baggage from childhood. To make matters worse, these pastors are wrapped in clerical robes and have the "authority of God" to give damaging counsel.

Zinnia came to see me simply because I am a woman. I am one who preaches about how professional counseling has helped me know the truth, and how knowing has allowed me to be set free. I have been trained through spending years in clinical pastoral education, both during and after seminary, which gave me further insight into my own dynamics and allowed me to work on myself. She had all of this information about me before she came. I also had the foresight to know that spiritual counseling would not render the freedom from fears that held Zinnia. I referred her to professional counseling and to a support group of women in our congregation for eight weeks.

Each of these activities gave Zinnia exposure to more social interactions. As the women began to share their experiences, Zinnia found herself able to relate and found that she was not the crazy, inadequate woman she had come to think she was. She was faithful in her attendance to the Listening Place (the name of our support group), as well as to her therapy sessions. She began to enjoy the times of sharing and receiving affirmations from others. In this milieu, she began to recognize her powers of selectivity and choice. One of the requirements for the eight weeks was to keep a journal of her progress, a written chronicle of each step of advancement. At the end of each session, we gifted ourselves with fifteen minutes of solitude for reflection and writing of thoughts and feelings. Zinnia worked herself through her pain. She did not "lose it."

We shared in that phone call, and I reminded her of other hurdles she had overcome. I listened to her fears and did not deny her feelings. Too often, we deny where a woman is, and in the process make her think she is crazy. Instead of giving her advice, I asked what she thought was the appropriate thing to do at this time. Within us is our every answer for guidance and instruction. Most of the time we simply need someone to listen to us and to help us clarify our thoughts. The next night the support group met for a dinner at a local restaurant.

Every time that we met, we would "check in," telling what we brought with us emotionally to this time of sharing. This allowed us to admit the space we were in and to receive caring, affirmation, and clarity for our journey. Sometimes the only response might be a smile, a touch, or a nod. But this night, just for Zinnia, we did something more. My secretary, Betty, had bought me a beautiful butterfly pin for my birthday. Butterflies are my symbol of freedom and continuing transformation. As I held the butterfly in my hand, I told Zinnia to hold onto the butterfly and to feel my love, strength, and positive feelings coming through to her whenever she felt she was losing it. Each one of the other women held the butterfly in their hands and gave her a gift to receive whenever she needed. It was a powerful moment of the transfer of our love to her.

The divorce is now final. Zinnia has endured much pain, humiliation, and frustration with a process that is not friendly nor geared to deal with the emotional needs of women. The emotional roller coaster has not completely leveled off to a smooth ride, and yet, Zinnia has not lost it. She has learned to reach out to other women, to get clarity of her thoughts, and to ask for help and support. We don't know what the end of this story is going to be, but we do know that much inner healing has taken place and that wholeness is a slow process, arrived at one step at a time.

GROWTH EXPERIENCES

1. If your story, like Zinnia's and Hagar's, involved rejection and its pain, you might want to spend time in meditation. To meditate is to cultivate the discipline of listening to, being made ready for, and practicing the presence of God. You might read a passage of scripture and then silently sit in reflection and allow the "spirit" of the passage to speak to your heart and mind. You may want to use a book of meditations to set the stage for being open to God in new and unexplored ways.

2. As your fears surface, allow the glow of God's love to surround each fear.

3. Listen for directions to guidance for relief. Let the light of God's love surround you. Know that you are loved and cared for by the One in whose image you are made. Bask in the sunlight of God's love for you often.

4. A book of guided imagery is helpful for assisting you with setting mental scenes for reflection and meditation. Books that have been helpful to me include *Imagine That* by Marlene Halpin, *The Woman's Book of Creativity* by C. Diane Ealy, *WomanWord* and *Woman Prayer, Woman Song* by Miriam Therese Winter, and *Simple Abundance* by Sarah Ban Breathrach.

5. Seek out a woman's support group. Adult Children of Alcoholics is a good beginning.

6. Call a woman whom you trust and ask her to share a meal with you. This may be the start of a relationship where you can listen to each other and be supportive.

7. Check the yellow pages for professional therapists. Remember that you have to interview them as well as their interviewing you! Select one whom you feel will listen to you and your concerns.

8. Begin to keep a journal for a dialogue with yourself. This journal can become the listening, nonthreatening friend you need. You can tell a journal your innermost secrets without fear of expo-

sure. The journal also becomes a record of each significant step that you have taken toward wholeness. When you feel that you are about to lose it, the journal becomes a reminder that this incident, too, will pass. See *Sister to Sister Devotions, Volume 2* and *The Companion Journal,* both by Linda H. Hollies and Judson Press.

3

step three

SHARING

have returned from visiting with Belle. She is a study of creativity in motion. For the past few years we have been sister-friends. Early in the morning and late at night we have talked on the telephone and shared our very lives. A major project that has impacted the lives of thousands of women was fleshed out and refined as we walked the track at the vocational school. We encouraged each other to lose weight and be healthy.

This visit was just for her. She was in much pain and distress, rejected by a man not even worthy of her attention. Once again we returned to the walking track to clarify some issues and make another attempt to be whole.

BELLE'S STORY

Belle is single and in her forties. She is a professional social worker with a master's degree and a brand new Saab. Blessed to have traveled the world extensively, she owns a delightful home filled with hospitality, love, and wonderful art. Statuesque, refined, and a trained wardrobe consultant, she makes an entrance that is unforgettable. To the world she looks like a woman who has it all. Yet Belle feels that God has punished her, rejected her, and left her alone. She has no husband and no children. She feels unfulfilled, empty, and alone.

Belle was born into the middle of a huge southern family, where there was always much noise and never enough attention for Belle. As with many daughters, she idolized her father, who was a struggling farmer and itinerant preacher. He was a tall man who seemed like a giant to Belle. Many evenings, when he had returned home, Belle would walk the fields, stepping deliberately into his footsteps that had been pressed into the dirt. In adulthood, she is still stepping into his footprints. Because she, like her father, is involved in the ordained ministry.

Her father was a man of few words and a quick hand. Struggling to make the ground produce food did not leave much time for long, leisurely father-to-daughter chats. His neglect burned into her soul. The need to have the approval and the love of her father has haunted Belle and overshadowed all of her relationships with males. Belle is continuing to seek that male companion who can fill the requirements of the long-sought-for relationship with her father. This quest is, of course, not a conscious decision. But Belle, like many women, is a vessel in need of inner healing.

God has blessed Belle with an exciting and creative ministry. She is a dramatist who can capture the very essence of a woman's soul. She has traveled the Midwest presenting dramas of historical women. Working in her local community she has developed a core of women who portray the lives of various women from the scriptures. They have performed at churches, college campuses, dinner theaters, and conferences. Belle researches, writes, and produces her monologues and their plays. This medium is her child. This the fruit of her womb. She is constantly pregnant and bringing forth life. Belle is busy, engaged with God in the creative order of spreading the good news with a new medium. Like Mary, Belle has been chosen to give new life in an unorthodox way.

MARY'S STORY: A UNIQUE BIRTH

The angel Gabriel found the virgin girl Mary, who was engaged to a man named Joseph. He greeted her with the words, "Greetings, favored one!" Does this not mean one who is enjoying or ready to enjoy God's special favor and presence? The angel hurried to assure her that "The Lord is with you!" A young, unmarried woman receiving the startling message of a forthcoming pregnancy would need this assurance and support. For like many of us, Mary found herself in a crisis. Her immediate response had to be fear. For the angel continued, saying, "Do not be afraid, Mary, for you have found favor with God." And now, you will conceive in your womb and bear a son, and you will name him Jesus" (Luke 1:28–31).

For centuries the children of Israel had looked forward to the promised Messiah. The Hebrew scriptures had foretold his glorious coming. But, how could this be happening to her, an unmarried virgin? How could she deal with the talk and the speculation? How could she explain this to Joseph? How could she convince a mere man, another human, to trust her explanation? And yet, she gave her consent. For

Mary knew that her baby was to be the very Son of God. Her son was destined for greatness. This child was to succeed the throne of David, but his reign would never die. His rule would last forever. When emperors, kings, pharaohs, and Herods had gone and left their glory behind, her baby would yet be reigning monarch throughout the ceaseless ages.

Mary was amazed. She asked one simple question, "How shall this be?" How is not the question of a doubter, but of a believer. For with the question, "how?" she had given her consent. Now, she wanted direction. It was then that the angel gave her further insight. "The Holy Spirit will come upon you, and the power of the Most High will over-shadow you; therefore the child to be born will be called holy, the Son of God."

When most of us receive word of how we are to be em-ployed in the ministry of spreading Jesus in our earthly realm, we immediately respond with "Why?" The why ques-tion always holds within it the element of argument and de-bate. The "why" has never been answered in the biblical record. The how question only gives assent and asks for clar-ification. God responds by giving good directions as the work of the Holy Spirit is to lead and to guide. It was the Holy Spirit, brooding, hovering, and wooing in creation, blessing everything in the created order with power to multiply, re-plenish, and to bring forth its own kind. That function is yet in operation. While we are busy, running around, trying to get God to do things our way, it is the power of the Holy Spirit that can put a yes to God's way deep down in the in-side of our soul.

As Belle can move from questioning her single, mother-less status in an argumentative manner and journey to a pos-ture of inquiring how she can live a productive and mean-ingful life as a single woman, direction will become more clear and her spirit will be more at ease. For it is the function of the Holy Spirit to generate the desire within you to love God so much until God's request of you is not grievous. The Holy Spirit will generate enough courage and fortitude that the fear is dissipated. The Holy Spirit will generate enough holy boldness within you that the traditional norms and standards of wifehood, motherhood, and apple pie do not matter. As we yield our lives to the leading of the Holy Spirit, our "why?" questions will become "how?"

Mary was selected to reproduce Jesus in the earthly realm. What we have here is an intimation of how the new creation story must first begin within us. Mary was chosen, in an unorthodox manner, to reproduce the hope of glory within her very being. This is the call of God to Belle. Her inner healing will come by following the example of Mary. For just as the Holy Spirit had overshadowed the old, chaotic world and brought the cosmos out of it, this same reproducing Spirit would overshadow Mary and will also overshadow Belle, giving order and pattern to what has seemed void, empty, and meaningless.

CHANGING THE WHY TO HOW

It is a great moment in our lives when we can cease to wrestle with our present state and learn to cultivate passivity and watch God work on our behalf. Belle walked with me as I learned this great lesson.

I was a seminary trained woman, with a burning desire to be ordained by my denomination. But ordination required that I relocate. Relocation meant moving a daughter who was entering her sophomore year in high school. I tried to enter the process in my present location, only to have every stumbling block available put in my path. I took the summer off to wait on God to work. I knew that my call to the ministry was authentic. I knew that the rumblings and stirrings inside of me were to be shared with the world. I had spent precious time and energy wrestling with God, demanding answers to my "whys?" Why did I have to relocate? Why were doors closed in my face? Why weren't things clear, simple, and easy for me? I never got an answer, only more frustrations.

Belle and I walked daily. Although at first it seemed I was going around in circles on the high school track, the walking brought clarity and new vision. Answers began to emerge from the stirrings and inner rumblings. I will never forget how the Holy Spirit overshadowed me and provided a unique ministry that did not require ordination but gave me credence within my denomination and access to women across a broad spectrum. This direction was given in response to the how question, not the why. The clarity was given as Belle and I walked and talked and shared this new vision for spreading Jesus among the folks in our world.

THE UNITY OF SISTERS

Gabriel directed Mary to go and to visit with her cousin, Elizabeth, so that her faith in God's power could be further confirmed. The Holy Spirit impregnates. The Holy Spirit generates our positive response. And the Holy Spirit is the agent of family perpetuation. I'm often surprised at how God, through the Holy Spirit, brings us into and keeps us in relationships as women/sisters/friends. Many of our relationships are strange and uncommon. And yet, God has made us family. In the community of faith we are paired as the beautiful and the plain; the intellectual and the less literate; the young and the not-so-young; mothers, widows, married, and single women; the well-to-do and the welfare recipient. Just like in our natural families, no sister is too ugly, too funny-looking, too sickly, or too worrisome. For a sister represents the perpetuation of our family. This sister says that our mothers and grandmothers and great grandmothers did not die in vain. Our family continues through each other.

When Mary got the news from Gabriel that she was going to have a baby, we have no record of her mother being available, but the angel told her news—her cousin/sister, Elizabeth, who had been barren, was expecting! Mary hurried to Elizabeth's house—to the embrace of family. When Mary walked through the door, there were no formal introductions, no conversation about health, weather, or news of home. Elizabeth, filled with the Holy Spirit, immediately responded to Mary's pregnancy. Elizabeth recognized Mary as the honored mother of the Messiah, without being told. Instead of any suspicion or jealousy there was a welcoming salutation. Elizabeth felt unworthy that Mary would come to visit her, but as she bolstered up Mary's faith, she was filled with the Holy Spirit.

THE MINISTRY OF SHARING

You cannot share nurture and support without being nurtured and supported in return. You cannot give ministry without being ministered to in return. As they shared together both were blessed and strengthened. This is the story of two sisters, sharing one another's burdens. Elizabeth was too old to be pregnant, and Mary was too single to be pregnant, according to the world's standards. But, here they were together, in community. We are in community by divine design. We need each other. God expects and desires us to support and affirm each other. We need sisters in our life. For when God selects us for a particular pregnancy, to reproduce Christ in an unorthodox manner, somebody else ought to be able to tell that you are divinely pregnant. Giving birth to Christ is not a secret affair.

Our ministry, vision, ideas, and dreams must be confirmed by our faith communities. Yet all of our pregnancies must not result in identical twins! Mary's baby was unique. Linda's baby is unique. And Belle's baby ought to be unique! Sameness is our idol, but God does not place great value in sameness. God is a master in creating and blessing diversity. No fingerprints are the same. No snowflakes are the same. No leaves off the same tree are the same. We have sanctified sameness in order to have control.

Belle must look beyond the limited scene of a husband, a baby, and the myth of "happily ever after." The right man might be on the way, and then again, he may never appear. Inner healing comes with acceptance of our present state. When Belle can appreciate that her singleness is yet blessed with creativity and the reproduction of new life through her monologues and dramas, she can open wide her arms to accept and embrace her giftedness.

When Mary left Elizabeth, she was better able to go back to Nazareth and to deal with the situation there. She had received good, pastoral care. She had been affirmed and confirmed. She had been strengthened by her sister. And she had to return to face the difficulty of home. We each have to leave the track of sharing and support and return home alone. We are responsible to come home and continue the ministry of perpetuating the family through the spreading of Christ where we live.

Mary was overshadowed because the blessings of creation needed to be duplicated, replicated, perpetuated, and passed on to the generations that would follow. And Belle is a part of that blessed process, as she gives birth to new life in every person she touches through her life. There is hope, there is light, and there is help.

GROWTH EXPERIENCES

1. If the story of Belle is yours, spend some time meditating on the Luke 1 scripture passage.

2. As you read the passage, substitute your name for Mary and one of your close friends for Elizabeth.

3. Find a place that is quiet and well lit, take your journal, and note the message of the angel to you.

4. Reflect on the times that you have felt the overshadowing of the Holy Spirit invading your being, impregnating you with an unorthodox manner of spreading the good news to those you influence.

5. What is the situation that is pressing on you at present?

6. Are you wrestling, and yet questioning "why?"

7. For the next few minutes, change that question to "how?" and note your response.

4

s t e p f o u r

CONFESSION

Briana has the sort of home that is the perfect retreat center: spacious, beautiful, serene, and quiet. Her decor is oriental and her guest room is in the rear of the house, where only the sound of the morning birds penetrates the peace. Often, when the cares of ministry have sucked me dry, I retreat to her place for restoration. She is Ms. Hospitality Plus, a giving and generous person.

Early one Saturday morning after a wonderful night's rest in her home, I awoke to sounds that were familiar, and yet strange in this environment. Briana was sobbing inconsolably. As much as she tried, no words would come in response to my questions inquiring what was wrong. I had never seen this side of Briana, and I could only sit with her and wait.

BRIANA'S STORY

This strong woman is a divorced, single parent with a daughter in college. She is an executive secretary for a major industry. For the past two years she has been involved in night classes to complete her undergraduate degree. Her plans are to attend seminary and become a professional minister. With this goal in mind, she has worked in her local church as an associate on the ordination track. Her pastor had asked for a meeting with her this morning. It was from this meeting that she had just returned.

Briana had gone to the church that morning, looking for her pastor to give her a glowing evaluation of her year's ministerial work. She needed him to say that she was indeed a wonderful minister. He let her know that she had not met his expectations. She was too aggressive, too assertive, and too boldly militant a woman for his taste. All of the achievements in her life threatened him. He declared her unfit for the ministry. He told her that he would not recommend her to the authorities for ordination.

Briana was crushed. She held her head high and made a graceful, "ladylike" exit. She gave him the very appearance of strength. But the pain of this rejection swelled up within her and mixed with the pain of the other rejections by significant men in her life. At home she began to lament her losses.

Things had not been easy in this pastor-associate relationship. This pastor was accustomed to women waiting for his direction. Women in the pulpit are a relatively new phenomena in most mainline denominations. It is into a complex set of dynamics that male pastors and female associates enter.

We each bring our personalities, our backgrounds, and often our unrealistic expectations of each other. Briana had looked to her pastor as a father figure, trusting him for direction, guidance, and mentorship. He had expected a "nice little woman" who would complement him, not upstage him, and be willing to allow his timing schedule to prevail. Both of them had unrealistic expectations. Both of them were disappointed.

Men have never met Briana's needs, beginning with her father. The youngest of two girls, she was raised by an alcoholic father and a mother who enabled her father to continue drinking. This dynamic, at work in many of our homes, set off a chain of needs, desires, and expectations that Briana has worked out of all of her life. Innately, there is the need to complete the relationship with our fathers. When we cannot do that as children, we unconsciously begin that search with other male relationships. Not having the necessary love, attention, and nurture from our dads, our sense of self-esteem is low. An alcoholic parent automatically triggers in us a sense of rejection and failure, as we work unendingly to "make them stop."

This pattern, set in childhood, continued to work as Briana found a man to marry who was similar in psychological makeup to her father. The old adage is that we seek an individual "just like good old dad." Even when dad is not good, we seek one like him. Needless to say, this relationship did not last long. Separation and divorce bring with them additional feelings of rejection, loss, and anger, which simple time lapse does not erase or dissolve. Briana, innocently enough, brought these feelings and expectations with her to the church. Too many of us turn to the church as an escape from our pain, only to discover that other human beings make up the church. When the church adds to our pain, we discover, like Briana, that we are vessels in need of inner healing.

HANNAH: FINDING SELF-WORTH

In the book of 1 Samuel we discover Hannah, a woman at odds with herself, her family, and her church. Hannah's problem was that she had no real sense of her self, her worthiness, and her inner beauty. Living in a male-dominated society, her roles and functions were decided for her. We learn of her role as wife to Elkanah, a wealthy man. The community expectation was that she was to bear children and assume the role of mother. A woman of this time period was only known as someone's daughter, wife, or mother, if she was a decent woman. So, as a married woman who did not have children, she was out of relationship with her community. She experienced rejection.

Hannah was also out of relationship with her sister. As the elder or first wife, she is known as the preferred wife. She was the ruler of the household. Scholars think that her husband took a second wife only due to her barrenness. Elkanah even told her that he loved her more than the other wife and more than his offspring. But, the fact that she could not have children became a point of scorn and put-down by the second, younger, fertile wife. Peninnah used her role as childbearing wife to make Hannah's life miserable. Scripture says that Hannah was the victim of constant, cruel teasing and ugly remarks, which caused her much grief.

We have a woman who was out of relationship with her inner, authentic self. She had never touched her inner core, her authentic essence. She was a woman so tied to her roles that she could not relate to herself as a person. Because of the inner struggles and pain, Hannah turned to her faith. In her condition of hurt and brokenness, she made her way to the temple to pray. Eli, the high priest, thought she was a temple prostitute. (Talk about adding insult to injury!) Yet this woman prayed in her heart. And after finding that her fasting and praying had not brought about the changes she desired, she began to sob and to cry inconsolably.

VENTING THE PAIN

The world of yesterday and our world today says, "Be strong, don't cry, keep a brave front, and never let them see you sweat!" Although it is true that the strong will survive, the strong are not promised the consolation of our God. In the Beatitudes (Matt. 5:3–12) Jesus taught us that there is blessed consolation and comfort if we dare to mourn, cry, and grieve. The Greek word used here for mourn refers to one who laments as if crying for the dead. When we come to the recognition of how great our losses are, there is need to grieve. Hannah was not afraid to allow sorrow to wash her soul with passionate lamenting.

Simply crying, however, is not going to give us the answers to our situations. There are many "crybabies" who never achieve a modicum of success in their lives. Hannah teaches us something about the emotional expression of our pain. As she cried aloud, the priest inquired of her distress. She shared both her pain and her request of God. She was able to look at her self-hatred as a barren woman in the light of God's love. Giving vent to pent-up emotions allows us to get them outside of ourselves. Inner, unexpressed pain becomes magnified larger than life. Any emotion that we feel we cannot express has the power to control us. When we arrive at the point of having to let it "all hang out," we can get a sense of how to handle these same emotions.

Hannah decided to take charge of her life. In the first chapter of 1 Samuel, verse 12, she prayed. In verse 16 she talked of her anguish and grief. In verse 17 she was assured by Eli the priest that God had heard her cry. In verse 19 she

did two things that we so often forget: she arose and wor-
shiped God. It was then that God remembered her. For after
she had prayed in faith and in confidence, emotionally expressed her pains, she then went home with both a new attitude and a new self-appreciation. Relaxed and feeling better
about herself, that night as she and her husband made love,
she conceived.

The issue of Hannah's self-esteem was on the line.
Women must face the reality that we often have to push past
the unrealistic expectations set for us by our culture. Much
of our self-esteem problems stem from the norms of society.
Our family may also contribute to our low self-esteem. We
are taught the rules and roles of women at our mother's
breast. We look to our fathers to affirm that we are wonderful, lovable, and significant. In our homes we get a sense of
whether or not we matter and make a difference in the world.
When family dysfunction retards our developing self-esteem,
we enter adulthood fractured and fragile. Roles cover our
hurts and allow us to separate from our inner self.

When we don't deal with our low self-esteem, we live on
the edge of life, always feeling as if we're about to lose control. To lose control is to overeat. To lose control is to be addicted to tranquilizers, drugs, alcohol, men, and even to the
church. To lose control is to be addicted to our chosen role
and to be a perfectionist, realizing that we're never quite
good enough. To lose control is to give authority to others
while seeking affirmation and self-esteem. To gain control we
need to grapple with our inner pain, to emotionally express
our hurt, and to look at alternative actions.

NAMING THE PAIN

Like Hannah, Briana emotionally expressed the pain of many
years. And, after crying, Briana arose.

Briana took a giant step on that day. She began to look at her unrealistic expectations of her pastor. She began to consider and to name what her needs were. She began to affirm her self, her accomplishments, and her goals for life. This scene with her pastor allowed her to evaluate how she continually looked to males for confirmation and direction. She reflected upon how she seemed to seek out men who were emotionally unavailable to meet her needs, like her father had been in her childhood. As she began to assess her life she was able to stroke herself for the gains she had made in spite of the pain of her past. In this time of articulation, Briana recounted her call to ministry. Like Hannah, she was able to look at herself in the light of God's love.

Naming her pain gave Briana new strength and new courage. This incident gave her the impetus to make plans for the actualization of her goals. Briana graduated with her undergraduate degree. She quit her job and enrolled in a seminary. She moved away from her family and friends and ventured out into the unknown to follow God's call to professional ministry. The journey has not been easy. She has changed pastors and even moved to a different jurisdiction of authority. However, her former pastor continues to malign her name with the new authorities. This has not unsettled her determination nor shaken her new self-esteem.

Briana is in transition: a new educational experience, a new location, new acquaintances, and a new and less secure financial position. Yet, she feels good about herself. She is able to reach out to others as she journeys toward inner healing. For on the same day that she emotionally expressed her pain, she arose—and God remembered her!

GROWTH EXPERIENCES

1. If your story sounds like Hannah's and Briana's, you need to rise up and claim your personal power.

2. Sit down and look back over your life. Go back in seven-year intervals.

3. Recount the significant losses, achievements, successes, and failures in each seven-year interval.

4. Write letters to significant individuals.

5. Stop and mentally revisit painful situations.

6. Grieve and say good-bye to necessary losses.

7. Find someone to share with you all the victories you have never celebrated.

8. Plan a "just because" dinner and invite significant women who will come and share as you celebrate yourself!

5

step five

RECONCILIATION

inda, when will my time come?" asked Shala. "I am tired of waiting and hurting and living with this old, haunting rejection. When will I be first choice to someone?" These are very important questions if we are going to face our reality and deal with the issues that bring about our inner pain. It had taken Shala over three years to come to the point of even raising these questions as we did walking therapy together.

SHALA'S STORY

I had met Shala about a month before her marriage. She and her fiance had called to ask me to do the premarriage counseling, since her pastor lived far away in her hometown. At our first session I knew that there was trouble. Alan's mother, dead father, and siblings were yet the primary influences in his life. Shala had her own problems, for she had just recently found out the truth about her birth mother's murder when she was five. Having been raised by a series of relatives, and having no relationship with her biological father, an alcoholic, her marriage was off to a very shaky start. At the end of our six sessions, my advice to this couple was to postpone the wedding, get individual therapy, and wait.

My counsel was not heeded. The marriage date had already been set for two weeks away, invitations had been mailed, and an expensive dress purchased. Egos and pride were factors to be dealt with. After the honeymoon and the first painful month, Shala called me again. A crowded schedule prevented me from having time to provide her with individual counseling. My own inner needs demanded that I walk for an hour daily to clear my own head and to meditate with nature. I told her that if she was willing to walk with me one day weekly, we could meet. Walking therapy began.

Shala is the oldest of two siblings, with three years between her and her brother. At age five their mother had died (so they were told), and the father was not in the home. The maternal grandmother raised them. However, two years later the grandmother died. The relatives contacted the father, who lived out of state, and the siblings began a series of moves with this man who could not maintain a job because of his drinking problem. Finally, amid much arguing and bickering, the paternal grandparents took both of the children. The grandfather was adamant that this was not the proper move, for they (the grandparents) were just beginning to "live." The grandmother was just as insistent that this was their reasonable duty. Into this home of divided opinion and covert resentment Shala and her brother moved just as she was entering puberty.

Shala, like many of us, felt rejected by her father who was, first of all, not in the home during her formative years. She knew that she was not his first choice. The maternal grandfather was dead, and death seemed like and felt like rejection. So, Shala was not this "father's" first choice. And, finally, the paternal grandfather was resentful of having to provide her a home. She was not his first choice either.

The book *Women Who Love Too Much* by Robin Norwood has provided much documentation about the emotional need women have to "find" their fathers in other significant relationships. It tells of how much pain we will bear, how long we will suffer, and how much we will deny our reality as we continue to search for this very important relationship.

I have learned from my training in clinical psychology and from my own personal experience that when the emotional bonding with our father is not available, we will unconsciously seek an individual who we can identify with as "good old dad!" We seek a nurturer, someone we can trust, and someone we can depend on to care both for and about us (like we believe that our father would have done). However, we usually select individuals who are just as emotionally unavailable as our biological father was. So, following true to course, Shala got involved with men who could not fill her emotional needs. Until Alan came along, she had been able to terminate relationships before marriage.

We need to understand the other significant individuals in Shala's development. At age five her mother died—rejection. Her maternal grandmother died two years later, another rejection. Finally, there was the paternal grandmother, who was available. She felt that it was her duty to raise these children. When Shala was twelve, her grandmother's brother began to fondle her and to make improper advances. Her grandmother dismissed Shala's complaints. When the uncle finally raped her and she told her grandmother, she told Shala, "We cannot tell anyone—it would cause too much family confusion!" Another rejection! Shala had been forced to internalize the compiled rejections, which felt like guilt, shame, and anger. These forces, turned inward, became a growing, gnawing, overwhelming depression that was not easily shaken.

Knowing that there was no one else to trust, feeling that she would not ever become number one with anyone, Shala took on the role of Super Achiever in order to prove herself worthy of love and acceptance. Not only did she care for herself, but she took care of her younger brother in order to "save" him. Academics and scholastic achievements became a way to prove tangible self-worth. After high school Shala went to college and earned a business degree. She interned for a Fortune 500 company's management training. But the outward trappings of success did not help the inner pain of not being first! She began to search for another company, another challenge, another place to prove herself. She was hired by a major automobile corporation and placed in an upper management position, where she met Alan.

During this period of searching for her place and forming her identity, Shala determined to discover as much as she could about her biological mother. She wanted to get to know her as a person, not as the "stories" she had heard for many years. She and Alan began a library research, and they visited the hometown of her mother as they became involved in a full-scale, "missing persons" mission. Shala and Alan dug and dug, and discoveries began to emerge. Her mother had been murdered. The newspaper account tied her to a pimp. The suspected pimp was none other than Shala's biological father!

These revelations caused Shala to question, "Has anyone ever loved me? Am I worthy of being loved, if this is the truth?" Alan responded in the affirmative, and an engagement was made. The wedding date was set, and the marriage began.

Shala was not tricked into marriage, but she tricked herself into believing that if Alan could love her, knowing about her past, then she was first with him. But as the tenderness and lovemaking of the honeymoon gave way to the dawn of the stark reality of daily living with another, Shala found once again that she was not first with Alan, not second, but a distant third.

Alan is a middle child, often called a "lost child" in family systems. He felt rejected by his deceased father and by his mother, who adopted three of her dead sister's children. What we had in this marriage arrangement were two very needy individuals, each seeking what the other could not give. When Shala did not become his "mother" and take away his pain, Alan turned heavily to drugs. In response, Shala did what many of us do, she turned to heavy denial. "It's the family's fault—if they would just leave us alone!" "If they would not put so much pressure on him at work." "He expected me to work, do all the cleaning, cook, and shop." The story is so familiar to women who continue to wait for this illusive thing called love and "being first."

Walking therapy allowed us to walk off much of the tension and frustration that Shala brought with her. It also gave me the space to listen and not be distracted by the normal office "stuff." I listened as she told her story. I asked questions to allow her to hear her own answers and clarify issues for herself. I have learned that when individuals view themselves as victims they will not accept your answers anyway. They will fight with you in order to prove how little you really understand their unique situation. I often asked Shala, "What did this particular choice give you?" I felt that Shala needed to be first with Shala, but in her searching she had neglected to find out who she was as a person, as a woman, as self. I refused to deal with Alan and Alan's issues. I did recommend that he return to therapy, but I refused to see him and referred him to a peer.

Shala was asked to keep a journal and was given a list of affirmations for women. The list contained much of Virginia Satir's philosophy in "My Declaration of Self-Esteem" (see the appendix of this book). I told her, "Tape them to your bathroom mirror. Tape them on the dashboard of your car. Keep a list in your desk drawer." Our focus became Shala and what she wanted to do for herself and with her life. Divorce was not mentioned, for that would have been another rejection, a way to get caught up in the same vicious cycle again. Shala had to make choices from a proactive stance—a difficult task for a people pleaser who has to be liked and accepted in order to feel worthy.

LEAH: A STUDY IN REJECTION

The Old Testament story of Leah, the wife of Jacob, is the story of rejection, pain, and a woman's reality of being her husband's second choice. Jacob, the main character in the twenty-ninth chapter of Genesis, makes no small matter of the fact that his love and his heart was knit to Leah's younger sister, Rachel. Just to set the story in perspective, it is necessary to let you know that he had worked seven years as a laborer for the father of these women in order to be given

Rachel as his wife. At the end of the agreed upon term, the wedding was arranged. As was the custom, the bride's face was veiled and her eyes were always downcast. Can you even begin to imagine the worry, frustration, fear, and anxiety of Leah as she was forced to be the stand-in at the wedding? At the insistence of her father she had been robed with the bridal attire and sent to wed Jacob.

The biblical record tells us that Leah had a condition of the eyes that made her less physically attractive than her sister, but custom dictated that the older sister wed first. So, she stood at the wedding feast, made her vows, and was led off to the bridal chamber for the consummation of the marriage. As the tenderness and lovemaking of the night gave way to the stark and naked truth of the dawn, how would Jacob feel about her? She already knew that she was not his first choice.

There are many women who are second choice in significant relationships. We seem to wait forever for the right love, the right man, or even the right time. We wait, embraced by loneliness, wrecked by inner pain and despair, kissed by fear, and caressed by anxieties. We wait, pleading to be someone's first choice, to be loved for who we are, not for what we can give. We wait and we hurt. We love and we long to be loved. And we begin to realize that our bodies, like Leah's, are not our own. We have been traded, bartered for, abused, violated, raped, married off, and taken advantage of, simply because we are women. And so, we wait.

Decision making is a difficult process under the best of circumstances for most women. For our decisions affect many lives, and relationships often entangle themselves into our choices. Leah, after this fateful encounter with Jacob, had some decisions to make. Her first choice was to win the heart of her husband through children. In Genesis 29:32, we find that Leah named her first child Reuben, and said,

"Because the Lord has looked on my affliction; surely now my husband will love me." It did not make her first with Jacob, for he continued to work for her father another seven years in order to marry Rachel as his second wife, his first choice. In verse 33, Leah named son number two Simeon and said, "Because the Lord has heard that I am hated, he has given me this son also." She was still her husband's second choice. In verse 34, she conceived again and named her son Levi: "Now this time my husband will be joined to me, because I have borne him three sons." Yes, the boys were favored by their father. But, no, their mother was not his first choice. Finally, in verse 35, Leah made a decision. She said, "This time I will praise the Lord." She named her fourth son Judah, which means praise.

RECONCILING THE PAST

Letting go of dreams and hopes causes us to reassess our priorities. This process is a transition period that offers no clear-cut paths, no crystal clear answers, and no guarantees of what we will find on the other side. All transitions require this period of fuzziness, trial, error, pain, and anxiety. For we know what we have experienced. We have some coping mechanisms to deal with what we can predict. Even though our reality might be filled with suffering, it is often because of our decision to remain in what is known, rather than venturing into the unknown. Shala had to come to the point where the pain of the unknown was less frightening than the pain of her reality. She had to journey through many difficult paths, avenues, and blind alleys as she sought relief and wholeness. But, like Leah, she decided to risk.

Her first decision to risk was simply facing the fact that she no longer needed a mother and father in the same way that she did as a little girl whose parents "rejected" her by death and abandonment. She had to learn to "reparent" herself and reprogram her parenting tapes, which continued to cause her seeking to be first with others. Her second decision was to work on Shala, to get to know, understand, and love herself. She began to do something nice for Shala on a daily basis. She began to plan her future in long-term goals with immediate steps to reach her goals. She enrolled in a Dale Carnegie course offered by her employer. Her self-confidence began to increase. She enrolled in a graduate school to obtain her master's degree. After two years she filed for divorce and left Alan in the apartment. Risky business, but she was determined to make Shala first in her life.

Shala moved in with a female friend in order to make the adjustment to single life a bit easier. She did not have an easy time adjusting. The question, "Did I do the right thing?" continued to haunt her for many days. She continued to move in the direction she had charted for herself. She continued to walk, talk, and share her pain. As women, we look for much from our relationships with other women. As Shala tried to cut the cord with her paternal grandmother, she tied herself to her roommate. Severing relationships that continue to cause perpetual pain should speak to us loudly and clearly, but ties between women are strong. Like Leah, Shala grew, changed, became different, and refused to allow another painful relationship to stop her progress.

Taking little steps, letting go a bit at a time, and encountering and surviving the grief helps us to make the bigger, more difficult leaps into wholeness. We find Leah again in Genesis, chapter 30, verse 9. Here she has made herself number one. Knowing full well that Jacob will never love her, but not having the privilege to divorce him, leave him, or ask him to leave, she made another decision. She gave Jacob her maid and made the executive decision to stop chasing that illusive rainbow. The key to this whole passage comes in verse 13: Leah said, "Happy am I! For the women will call me happy."

Even this story does not have a happily-ever-after ending. There were other choices and other decisions Leah made that resulted in two additional sons and a daughter by her husband. The relationship between her and her sister was never made right because of the initial arrangements made by their father. Leah did learn, however, how to value her authentic self and to make peace with her past. She understood that hoping, wishing, and dreaming fantasies did not make reality. She began to think of herself and her needs. Because she came to a point of peacemaking with her life, she has an unequaled place in the history and life of Jesus Christ: Her husband's name was changed to Israel, and Jesus Christ was born of the tribe of Judah, the chief of praise. Leah did not give birth to Judah until she began to recognize and to separate her identity from that of her father, her husband, and even her sister. She began to search within for her own identity and peace.

The lessons of our life are hard-earned and not easily or quickly learned. Thank God for time! Shala did complete graduate school. She did get involved with another male who was asking too much of her and was unwilling and unable to give her much in return. She broke off the relationship. She decided to ask for a transfer to another city, which meant leaving the place of work where Alan remained, severing ties with the female roommate, and leaving her comfort zone of social ties and connections. But Shala says that she is now numero uno and she is taking leaps of faith to prove it to herself. She has moved into an apartment of her own and is venturing out, seeking to establish new networking contacts. Her brother recently married and moved far away, and she was able to rejoice in his leavetaking. She did not move back into the city where her grandparents reside. She has begun to challenge her grandmother about the lifestyle that she is trapped in. Shala continues to be involved in support groups to help her deal with being the adult child of an alcoholic as well as an incest survivor.

Although we are miles apart, we maintain a close relationship. Recently, when I went through another one of life's frequent challenges, it was a card and words of wisdom from Shala that allowed me to see that life does go on, in spite of the pain of letting go of dreams, hopes, and fantasies. To me this is the proof of Shala's coming of age. She is now feeding me back my own counsel. Those of us who know her and know how far she has traveled can testify that inner healing is well on the way. Letting go of a stunting, retarding past is in process. We look at Shala and listen to her reports of new life and know that we can call her "happy."

GROWTH EXPERIENCES

If your story sounds similar to Shala's, here are some things you can do to make peace with your past and come to the point of saying, "Now I will praise the Lord!"

1. In order to get to know yourself, find a place of retreat, meditation, or solitude.

2. Plan one day a month just for you! If you can find a spiritual director to help you formulate your day and to be a listening ear and reflector, you can begin to strip away the layer of expectations, roles, and fantasies that you have operated from in the past.

3. A journal of accomplishments and feelings is a must. You can write out what you may often not be able to articulate to another. But as you write openly and honestly the feelings you are experiencing, it will become easier to share later.

4. Find a list of positive mental attitude tapes and affirmations and give yourself the gift of at least fifteen minutes daily to talk to yourself, thus reprogramming your tapes. The books *Showing Mary* by Renita Weems and *Prayer, Stress, and Our Inner Wounds* by Flora Slossom Wuellner will provide many salient and helpful pointers if you are not currently in therapy or in a support group.

5. A step group for adult children of alcoholics and incest victims provides a warm, nonthreatening atmosphere that allows for growth.

6. Get outside and walk at least twenty minutes daily. Really see the fine, accurate, and beautiful details of leaves, plants, and nature in general. Know that if there is a God who loves beauty so much that the seasons come for our enjoyment, this same creative God has planted beauty down within you.

7. Both of my parents are dead. And yet, for me to make peace with my past, I have had to go and visit the cemetery and "talk" with them. It gave me a great release from holding on to pain,

anger, hurt, and resentment. I needed to say these things aloud. Try this for yourself.

8. You may need to first write your feelings in your journal and then state them honestly. Letting go of pain is not letting go of love. It is declaring that you are now in the place and time where you can provide gentle, loving, and even corrective parenting to the little girl that continues to live inside you.

6

step six

CHOOSE TO BE DIFFERENT

Carla comes from a home with a very reserved and withdrawn mother and a father who was a workaholic. Feeling the need to win their love and attention, Carla took on the role of super achiever in the family. She was a brilliant student and won high scholastic honors. College was considered the proper thing to do and a career in finance became her objective. Completing the task of being awarded CPA certification was a great achievement, but Carla still felt that she did not measure up. She continued to search for other ways to prove herself worth loving. In college she met the man who was to become her husband, and they planned for a big family. She set aside her career and became Mrs. Carla, the homemaker.

Carla was born during the period when it was not considered proper to try to "have it all." A woman's place was in the home. She set forth all of her efforts and energies toward being a good wife and trying to become a mother. When the first year went past and she was not pregnant, the questions from family and friends began in earnest. With the passing of the second year, her husband and she began to worry about her fertility. The ghost of her past became a haunting presence—"You are not worthy!" Doctors, charts, graphs, and home remedies became a way of life as she and her husband tried every known measure to get her pregnant. There are many factors that can prevent pregnancy, including a male's sperm count. However, Carla was brought up during an age when women took all of the blame and carried all of the guilt for situations like these.

The deaths of her parents came during these troubled years, and feelings of guilt, loss, and rejection were multiplied in her life. Marrying a man who was emotionally like her father did not help an already tense and frustrating situation. Her husband was able to hide from his pain by becoming more and more involved in affairs. The whispering began, and soon echoes of another woman reached Carla. To further complicate matters this woman had a child. Carla's world was shattered when her husband asked for a divorce. It seemed that all was lost. She had been rejected by her parents, and now her marriage was a failure. Depression became her constant companion.

Working became a necessity and a way of escape from the pain of being a failure. Carla returned to school to update her skills and began the difficult process of searching for a new position after years away from the workplace. During this period she was invited to a woman's Bible study group, which became a place of support and friendship. She joined the church and became more socially involved than she had planned to be. Securing a position in a local bank seemed to give her a well-rounded and balanced life. Yet something was missing.

There was a new man, a new courtship, the revelation of previous pain, and the decision to marry again. This time Carla decided to continue to work while trying to get pregnant. After two years the couple decided to adopt. They adopted a son, and two years later, a daughter. Life seemed so complete. Once again, Carla left the work force in order to give her family what she had never received: love and complete acceptance. The children were the objects of her affection and attention. Her spouse found diversions, and once again the story of "another woman" began to surface. The inevitable divorce followed, but Carla felt secure with her children.

Children have a way of growing up and away from us, regardless of how attentive and loving we might be to them. Activities, friends, and school took the children, and once again the pain of rejection surfaced. For the third time Carla returned to work and church activities to fill the aching void. To make matters worse, her daughter began to question her about her "real mother." The relationship grew more and more stormy as the child grew into the teen years. When her son left for college, Carla thought the breech between her and her daughter might be mended. But the pain of rejection in her daughter was as strong as her own. During the last two years of high school, her daughter intensified her search for her birth mother, which made Carla feel more and more rejected.

Carla's friends in the Bible study group sustained and supported her during these painful years. She found herself turning more and more toward her faith to carry her through. One year on retreat she strongly felt a call to ministry. An overwhelming sense of being loved and accepted by Christ matched nothing that she had ever experienced. As she shared with her retreat companions, they encouraged her to follow her sense of call. But the old tapes began to play, "You are not worthy!" As she returned home to the empty nest, these old and familiar feelings seemed to dismiss what she had felt and experienced on retreat. By now her daughter was in college also, and their separation seemed complete. Her son's school involvement and summer internships kept him busy most summers, and the feelings of rejection and worthlessness drummed louder and louder in Carla's ears.

THE WOMAN AT THE WELL: FEELING UNWORTHY

As I listened to Carla's story I was reminded of a biblical sister who must have had similar feelings of unworthiness and aloneness on her journey. We know her as the woman that Jesus met at the well in the Gospel of John, chapter 4. We find this sister coming to Jacob's well at high noon, all alone. In the hot, eastern countries, it was the custom for women to journey together to the wells for the daily supply of water. They made it a time of socialization early in the morning before the sun was too high and the weather too hot. But, due to this sister's reputation, the women did not want to associate with her. She was not a mother like them. She was considered unworthy.

What amazes me in this passage of scripture is that it is the longest, most comprehensive piece of dialogue that we have recorded of any individual's conversation with Jesus. Our sister was a Samaritan, considered unclean by Jews, for her people had intermarried with foreigners. She was a female, and regardless of the ethnic group, women were considered inferior and viewed only as property. She was to be exchanged for goods in marriage, able to bear children, keep a decent home, and do as she was told. And yet, Jesus sat on the well and had a theological dialogue with this sister.

Most of us have heard this story taught as the woman with loose morals, for she is recorded as having had five husbands, and at the time of her conversation with Jesus, she was unmarried, living with a man. She had no children that we know of, her reputation was tarnished, and the women of the city had nothing to do with her. Pain and guilt must have been her constant companions. She was not considered "normal," or part of the status quo. But Jesus recognized her inner pain and emptiness. To have one husband walk off and divorce you is a traumatic event to any one of us today. But we cannot even begin to comprehend the customs that dictated that a woman return home to her parents, her father or male relative beginning again the bartering system of acquiring a dowry. A woman had no rights and could not file for a divorce. All a man had to do to divorce a woman was to file his petition of complaint with the city elders and to publicly declare his intention to divorce. Consider the pain of having to live through this hurt and rejection for a total of five times and to be blamed for your situation. For the act of burning the soup a man could divorce his wife, be relieved of his responsibilities, and leave her in disgrace.

As Jesus and this sister talked about the living water that would quench her thirst, he invited her to go and get her husband so that he could also receive this gift. And out of forty verses of dialogue, three verses are set aside to deal with the matter of her living conditions. In verses 17 and 18 we find these words: "You are right in saying, 'I have no husband'; for you have had five husbands, and the one you have now is not your husband. What you have said is true!" And, our sister replied, "Sir, I see that you are a prophet." End of conversation about the men in her life. I believe that with these words Jesus penetrated beyond our sister's mask and entered into the place of secret pain she carried. He recognized that rejection and guilt cause pain. He did not condemn her but pointed out that she was living with another man who was going to hurt her and cause further pain and rejection. This man (just like the other five) was not concerned for her welfare and well-being. He simply cared for what he could get from her.

They went on to talk about true worship in great detail. And in verse 26 Jesus revealed to her what he had not openly revealed to even his disciples: his messiahship. A deep conversation took place between Jesus and this woman whom the world judged unworthy and unlovable. Many great truths were revealed to her on that day. So great was the release of her pain and feelings of unworthiness that she chose to go back into the city, to those men and women who had rejected her, scorned her, and denied her access to social events. She became the first evangelist to the Gentiles and was quite effective. For in verse 39 it says: "Many Samaritans from that city believed in him because of the woman's testimony, 'He told me everything I have ever done.'"

Our sister made a conscious decision to put the pain of her past where it belonged—in the past. She chose to allow a new lease on life to generate her different reaction to win those who were lost. Putting pain in the past is a necessary step to inner healing. This sister, like Carla, had to work through her painful past by confronting the very persons who hurt her the most. Sometimes we have to do this by writing letters to those who are deceased, sitting at the gravesides, or returning to the scene of the pain with those who are yet alive. Carla had to write letters to her parents and talk about the pain of a mother who was emotionally unavailable to her and a father who gave himself to work and did not share his life with an emotionally starved little girl who needed his love and attention. Carla had to confront both husbands, number one and two. She had to share her hurt, frustration, and anger at being cheated on, at being made to feel less than adequate for not being able to have children, and being left for another woman.

CONFRONTING THE PAST

This time of talking was not easy or painless for either party. We must learn to release the past and to speak of the former unmentionables. That which we cannot talk about controls us. When we can begin to talk about the pain, get it outside of ourselves, and allow the light and life of grace to touch it, we can begin to control our emotions and not react to the former dominion of our hurts.

Carla's most difficult talk was with her daughter. She released much inner anguish by talking about the hurt and frustration of being a mother who had given all she had, nurtured as much as was humanly possible, and loved with all that was within her—only to have been dismissed because she was not the birth mother. Talking does not solve all of our problems, but it is a beginning point on the way to wholeness.

Now Carla's daughter has found her biological mother and is in a relationship with both of her mothers. Carla's son has married and he and his wife and children are holiday visitors with "Gran." Sharing her pain and returning to her place of call and retreat gave Carla the courage and strength to say yes to ordained ministry. At the ripe age of fifty, Carla enrolled in a seminary and completed her degree requirements for ordination. I got a call from her just before the ceremony: "Guess what? I just spent a fortune on all white underclothes. I realize that I am worthy! I have said yes to Jesus and good-bye to my feelings of unworthiness!"

Carla is a much loved and respected pastor. She is able to share her journey and life process with women in her congregation. One of the things I admire about her is her constant return to times of retreat. She heeds the voice of Jesus saying, "Come away awhile." She has begun a woman's Bible study group to offer a place of support and friendship to all women in her community and takes them on a quarterly retreat. Her pain at not being able to bear children and feelings of rejection and unworthiness are issues that she now uses to bless other women with the knowledge she has gained.

One year, just before the rush of Advent began, she called a group of female clergy together for a retreat, utilizing the spiritual direction of a Catholic nun. The focus for that retreat was to read the first chapter of Luke, verses 26 through 56. We were to "hear" the angel speak to us with a message of good news and write and reflect in the solitude. Because Carla found solace and a call to service in a retreat setting, she has provided these settings and opportunities for many of us. I was blessed tremendously and continue to return to my notes of that retreat.

Scars, wounds, and hurt make up the real and authentic Carla. Her pain of rejection and her barrenness have made her a caring and sensitive "mother" to women across denominational lines. She has nurturing tendencies and a warm and generous heart that is willing to share. I'm glad she traveled to the point of shedding the outer garments of despair and putting on the undergarments that symbolized for her the acceptance and love to be found in serving Christ through serving others in ministry. Carla is a vessel of beauty and great worth in the kingdom of God.

GROWTH EXPERIENCES

1. If your story sounds like Carla's and you have lived a life of seeming barrenness, find a quiet place and reflect upon the story of the woman at the well in John 4.

2. Have a long and intense conversation with Jesus, and let him touch you at your place of inner pain.

3. Focus on where most of your hurt and anger is centered and realize who it is you need to face, confront, and share painful feelings with.

4. Journaling the dialogue will give you many helpful insights.

5. Call a nearby Catholic retreat center and ask for help in locating a spiritual director. Let the director assist you in planning a day of retreat to begin the process of solitude and reflection.

6. If you are a woman who has been unable to bear a child, begin the reflective process of seeking to understand when you have been pregnant with ideas, plans, visions, and dreams.

7. How did you feel in the initial stages of carrying around these secret seeds, allowing them to germinate and grow?

8. Think of the many stages of growing and developing that you underwent in order to give birth and new life to a creation that now has been born.

9. Who were the midwives to your birthing process?

10. Who were those who encouraged you, prompted you, and helped you to pant and push when the pains of giving birth to a new creation caused you to consider aborting your dream? Giving birth to a natural child is an important process, but it is not the only birth process God calls us to be involved in. The continuing process of co-creating is yet our mandate and our innate desire. Let your birthing process begin!

7

step seven

CHOOSING DAILY

Proverbs 31 is usually the scripture I am given when church women call me to preach for a Woman's Day Celebration. This chapter asks the question in verse 10: "Who can find a virtuous woman? for her price is far above rubies" (KJV). I have refused to preach from this particular passage. I have some wonderful messages on biblical women and would take one of them to fit the occasion and theme. When I preach, especially to women, I try to preach from my own experiences, which I can relate to the scripture.

I just could not relate to this "virtuous woman" stuff! She sounded like a wimp—a little, meek, mild-mannered do-gooder. A virtuous woman sounded like a sweet, aged, stooped-over woman who knows her place and quietly and passively plays out her assigned roles in life. In the African American church, on Women's Day, the women all dress in white, from head to foot, looking prim, proper, and pure. These images just didn't fit my reality.

LINDA'S STORY

I am the survivor of incest by my father since the age of thirteen. My mother denied the dysfunction in our home and sacrificed me for her role as a wife. At the age of eighteen I married my high school sweetheart in order to escape home and took my dysfunctional dynamics right along with me. There was never any hope for the blossoming of this relationship, for I was determined that no man would ever control me, tell me what to do, or give me orders. I could not compromise, for I felt that I would forget my childhood experiences and become a weak woman like my mother. This meant that the birth of my two sons caused another battleground, for no one was going to take advantage of my children. Fighting within and fighting without does not allow one the privilege of being weak, mild-mannered, or pious.

Divorce. Painful relationships. Fading hopes and broken promises. Disappointments and rejections. This was my reality. I thought this was the way life was supposed to be, a daily struggle. I never knew inner peace, only inner brokenness.

I took the boys to church, but I could not relate to a male God who would take charge of my life, control my destiny, and cause me to be a weak woman, willing to be ordered around. So church involvement was out. My theme song became "My Way." Regardless of who was hurt, what had to be done, how I had to scheme in order to achieve the ends, I was going to do it my way. No meek, mild-mannered Linda was ever going to be seen. All relationships were war zones. I did not realize that my reactions to life were coming from my replaying the tapes from my childhood. Everything I despised about my father became operative in my way of relating to others. I felt that it was control or be controlled, hurt or be hurt. Virtue had nothing to do with my life—it was only survival of the fittest.

My aggressive attitude carried me from working as a local clothing store clerk to the quality control department in the steel mill. With educational benefits available there, I enrolled in college, while continuing to work full time. It was during this period that three important and life-changing events turned the course of my life. I met and married Chuck, we had a daughter, and I met Dr. Della Burt.

Charles Hollies was a supervisor in the mill. He was so different from the norm. He was a gentle, soft-spoken, and caring individual who only had one problem: he drank too much. But I felt I could change that! I didn't know that when one's relationship with her biological father is incomplete, she will seek out a man to fill this void. My father was emotionally unavailable to me, and when Chuck drank, he was also. Again I was married to a man that I could not "hear." And, as much as I loved him and he loved me, I could not understand the constant struggles in our relationship. If only he would stop drinking, everything would be perfect, I thought.

Our daughter, Grian Eunyke, became the motivation to change my life. Here was a miniature Linda who needed a role model as well as a mother. I wanted to show her how to live, but I had never learned to master life. I thought education, a professional position, and material things were the way to happiness, success, and inner peace. I quit my job at the steel mill in order to complete college degree requirements and to get on with life.

Taking an elective called "Black Women in Literature," I met Dr. Della Burk. Della—petite, single parent of one daughter, dreamer and risk taker—became a strong force in my life. As I read, studied, and listened to the life of other African American women, I began to understand that there was another way of living and relating to the world. It was in this period, so long ago, that I dared to be vulnerable enough to share my story with Della and to listen and learn from her. She was working as an adjunct professor while teaching full time in the public school system. The opportunity came for her to return to school and complete degree requirements for her Ph.D. That decision meant risk, taking her daughter and moving miles away from familiar surroundings and quitting a tenured position for the unknown of the future. Her dream was bigger than the risk, and off to school she went. She became my idol and my vision stretcher.

While taking additional writing courses, I was assigned to do an autobiography. For the first time I came face to face with my inner pain and the dysfunction that controlled my life. I knew something had to change, but I didn't know where to turn except to the church. So, with full force and enthusiasm, I returned to the God I had been running away from for years. Talking with my male pastor did not provide me with much relief, for he had not been trained in counseling procedures and could only offer me prayer. I thought that prayer was to be an instant cure for my pain and when this did not work, I thought it had to be my fault. I left his office feeling that either God would not listen to someone as "dirty and impure" as I was, or that God didn't care. Many years passed with my attending church, yet feeling critically wounded and empty. A male God just couldn't meet my needs.

Childhood issues do not leave us simply because we grow older. We continue to re-create our family's dysfunction and our roles of survival wherever we go. Family systems theory has taught me that the primary role of the family is to teach us intimacy, autonomy, trust, acceptance, love, communication skills, and how to share power. It is in our family of origin that we learn how to understand, value, and develop healthy body images and concepts. In my family this learning didn't happen. I aged, but I was developmentally retarded. I have come to realize that church can become an addictive crutch for people like myself. The church gave me a place of acceptance and the ability to work in areas where I once again misused my power. I began to look to a power outside of myself for guidance, but prayer alone was not my cure.

Success, good positions, and the accumulation of "things" made me feel that I was coping quite well. But the inner woman still felt unfulfilled, empty, and unclean. In the midst of this confusion I began to be aware of God's call to ministry. The questions about my past haunted me. The questions about being a pure, clean, chaste, and humble woman troubled me. The call was louder than my doubts, and I began to explore the possibilities of entering the ministry. After much talking with my family and friends, my pastor, and other ministers, it was determined that I should attend a seminary. (Talk about transitions!) My older son was out of school and working. The younger son was away in college. It was decided that thirteen-year-old Grian would migrate to our new home with me. Chuck was to remain in our family home, caring for my grandmother and working to pay the bills.

Seminary has a way of challenging your assumptions about life, as well as your faith. During my second year, all of the rumbling questions of my past came straight to the forefront. I was walking a fine line, hovering on the edge.

Garrett-Evangelical Theological Seminary in Evanston, Illinois, has a fine pastoral counseling program and makes it available to students in crisis, free of charge. Until seminary, I had never heard of pastoral counseling, clinical pastoral education, or chaplaincy training. I took advantage of these resources and found the help I had been needing for years.

I had taken a course during the summer called Clinical Pastoral Education, where I worked as a chaplain intern at a local hospital under supervision of a trained pastoral educator. Here is where the initial awareness of my dysfunctional family became clear. It was also here that I was cleansed from the guilt of feeling that I had seduced my father. This was the greatest relief; all of my life I had carried around this burden of guilt. It was here that I was referred to therapy, and because I wanted to be healed, I began to seek a therapist.

I was no longer able to hide from the fact that Chuck was an alcoholic. Once again I had to face the truth of having made a terrible decision for marriage. This was the first step of facing my past and its hold on my life. Finding a white, ordained feminist for a counselor was a freeing experience. Rev. Dr. Peggy Garrison helped me see that getting a divorce was not the only answer, but that I had serious choices to make if I wanted to begin the healing process. Continuing with therapy and training in Clinical Pastoral Education have been my salvation. I came to understand that I had to change my mental tapes and reparent myself. I had to face the truth that my mother chose to be a woman and a wife before being a mother. I had to face the fact that I could not relate to a male God image, for it always took me back to my father. A female God was also weak and powerless. I had to get away from a God of gender!

My last year of seminary was one of the most traumatic periods of my life. I began to serve as pastor of a small congregation in Lansing, Michigan. Chuck retired, and Grian transferred schools. I would take the train into Illinois on Monday afternoon and return to Michigan on Friday morning. We lived in the parsonage in Lansing, and I had an efficiency in Evanston. Three weeks before my final quarter, Chuck passed out behind the wheel of the car while returning Grian to Lansing. I gave him an ultimatum: enter an alcohol treatment center or divorce. He chose the treatment center, but insisted upon entering one close to the seminary. I was angry, resentful, and embarrassed. We celebrated our anniversary in the treatment center that year. While confined, Chuck came face to face with his alcoholism and turned his life over to Christ. His counselor tried to get me to enter codependency counseling, but I refused, feeling that only Chuck had a problem. For the rest of the year we walked on egg-shells around each other, afraid to be honest and frightened to death of a relapse.

With so much pressure mounting, I left the pastoral counselor and began to see a female psychoanalyst. One morning in April I awoke from a horrible dream in which I knew that my mother wanted to die. As I shared with the analyst the circumstances of my painful childhood and the rejection I felt from my mother, some fantasies and wishes I had carried for years began to die, too. The very next month my mother had a massive stroke and lingered in a coma until one week after my graduation. My father had died several years earlier, and all of a sudden, I realized that I was an orphan. Overpowering depression took control. I quit the pastoral assignment and took the summer off to think things through. As I walked and meditated, I realized how much I wanted to be free of the limits of my past. I finally made the decision to learn as much as possible about what made me the way I was. I wanted to know who I was. I decided to return to school again!

The closest center for training in pastoral clinical education was seventy-eight miles away in Ann Arbor, Michigan. But the information I needed was worth the trip. The department manager, Dr. Dennis Kenny, was a man who went straight to the heart of issues, and I didn't approve of his teaching methods. My first supervisor, Rev. JoClare Wilson, was just as tough, but I could take it from a woman. Our relationship was tenuous and stormy. There were many days that I could not discern whether my pain was from my past, my present, my race, or my gender. It was a difficult process, but I was determined to learn about Linda.

There are no words to explain the awesomeness of coming to realize who you are and the reasons for your reactions. I can only relate to you that one gray November day, as I sat in the hospital chapel, I came to understand that my mother could not have taught me about life and its beauty, its colors and brightness. My mother had never known this truth herself. It was at this time that I decided to stay after my intern year for a year of supervisory training, so that I could help other women find the beauty in life. Like Jacob in the Bible, I wrestled and I wrestled until I was blessed in the exchange. Every encounter brought me closer to freedom and healing, every student taught me how to experience grace. When my Annual Conference called to ask me to take a church in Illinois, I knew that I was ready to pastor. My own inner healing was well underway.

My last year in Ann Arbor, as I worked with students and shared with my peers and supervisors, I began a project to discern how I had made such tremendous movement toward inner wholeness. Many hours of dialogue, critical reflection, and honest sharing provided the chronological steps I had worked through. The last step was a progressive step, for it required choosing daily to journey toward inner healing and wholeness. Choosing daily means facing the evil without as well as the evil within. Deciding to choose meant that when I was asked this year to preach on the virtuous woman, I said yes to the challenge.

THE VIRTUOUS WOMAN: A WOMAN OF FORCE

The thirty-first chapter of Proverbs is a portrait of the ideal. It begins with a mother's prophecy being conveyed to her son, the king. We have no record of who King Lemuel might have been, but the name Lemuel means, "dedicated unto God." Most scholars have determined that this material is addressed to an ideal king, by his ideal mother, about an ideal wife. What was of extreme importance to me was the fact that this chapter is a prophecy, an oracle, or the teachings of a mother to her son. What? A woman giving a prophecy in the Old Testament?

We are told in verse one that this is an inspired utterance, a massa, or the anointed Word of God, given as maternal counsel. It begins with an exhortation to chastity, warnings against drinking and alcoholism, and demands that the king always be righteous in his judgments. These first nine verses establish the bridge, the link between the time this was written and the contemporary times in which we live. What the queen was essentially saying to her son is what Aretha Franklin tried to say to men in the early seventies: "If you want a do-right woman, you have got to be a do-right man!" For a virtuous woman was not the weak, meek, mild woman I had seen in my mind. The Hebrew for virtuous woman is ishshah chayil, a woman of force!

A woman of force is one who recognizes and celebrates her personal power. A woman of force is one who is busy working, knowing that she is girded with God's strength and vigor, which allows her to operate with ease and freedom. A woman of force is one who is living the abundant life, not tied to the limitations of her past. A woman of force is full of good works and charity. A woman of force is one who loves and reveres God. A woman of force shall be praised. Her own works and deeds will praise her. She is trustworthy. She is faithful. She is sympathetic. She is intelligent and industrious.

She is a woman of thrift. She knows the art of "stretch and make do." A woman of force is one who is gracious in speech and deliberate in her actions. A woman of force is one who has a personal, intimate relationship with God. She relies on God's strength. She relies on God's wisdom. A woman of force is Spirit-filled, Spirit-led, and Spirit-controlled. She has the fruit of the Spirit operating and evidenced in her life. She walks tall. She speaks with wisdom and the authority of God. She is a teacher. She is a leader. Other women look up to her. For she is known as a choice jewel among God's resources.

You have to take your hat off to this sister! She is a manager. She is the woman who is capable of doing what she needs to do, and doing it well. This was the first liberated woman! Without even a woman's movement behind her, she is a woman full of self-confidence and assurance. She is not swayed by circumstances nor moved by new situations. She is determined and fortified by the grace of our God. Of course her price is high! She is more precious than any fine jewel. Of course a man would have to travel to the ends of the earth seeking such a rare individual. What the mother said to her son, the king, was that this caliber of woman would not be easy to find, but she would be worth the search!

Who can find a virtuous woman? Well, I have the answer to this ancient question: I am one of them! And there are many more on the scene. I laugh at the sense of humor that God often displays to get our attention. Even while I was yet wrestling with whether or not to preach this text, the church that had invited me sent the information to the local newspaper. The week before I was to speak, my picture was in the paper. Under my picture was my name. Under my name were these words: A VIRTUOUS WOMAN!

How prophetic! How accurate! This is inner healing! For I am a woman of strong force, a power to be reckoned with, for I stand on the authority of my call to ministry. I utilize the pain, the scars, and the brokenness of my past in order to forge new avenues of hope and healing for others. A woman of force takes the stuff of the past and uses it instead of allowing it to use her! Every day I choose to say yes to the call of God on my life. Every day it is not easy. But next to my bed is a framed declaration of my daily choice to journey toward a more perfect and full inner healing. It is a gift given to me by my last class of students, and it says:

I'll say yes, Lord, yes!
To your will and to your way.
I'll say yes, Lord, yes!
I will trust you and obey.
When your Spirit speaks to me
With my whole heart I'll agree.
And my answer will be,
Yes, Lord, yes!

GROWTH EXPERIENCES

1. An important step in the process of inner healing requires that you make a conscious decision to develop good self-esteem. You must sincerely desire to feel and to think differently about yourself. You must realize and affirm that you are a divine design, created by a loving God.

2. Accept yourself. Acceptance of self will assist in the acceptance of others. Empathy can strengthen acceptance of others; it may result in understanding others' behavior. Self acceptance may be enhanced by spending time alone, getting to know your inner self, the authentic self, and cultivating qualities you admire in others.

3. Another effective method in raising self-esteem is praise. When you perform a task well, praise yourself by telling yourself, "I did a great job!" Seek your positive characteristics and actions, and stroke yourself when you exhibit these traits. Praise others; it has a circular effect. Before long, others will be praising you. Self praise will improve your self-dialogue, the manner in which you speak and think of yourself. Positive self-dialogue allows you to guide yourself through a "practice run" in your mind before you attempt to handle a problem.

4. Establish a useful goal-setting system that allows you to complete projects, jobs, and tasks with a high ratio of success. Set goals that are attainable but challenging at the same time. Take into consideration your past performance and competencies. Set small steps toward a final goal. Monitor each step. Reward yourself.

5. Atmosphere—including your physical, mental, and emotional surroundings—affects your self-esteem. The physical arrangement of your home should be clean and comfortable. A good mental climate affords stimulation that is challenging but not overwhelming. A supportive emotional atmosphere is essential.

6. Evaluate your bad habits. Study the habit, name it, claim it, and then re-aim that energy in stopping that action. Understand

what situations trigger the bad habit. Then stop, cold turkey! You will need continued awareness of the habit even after it is stopped in order to control not picking it up again.

7. Depression can damage self-esteem or can be a result of low self-esteem. For some women, depression may require professional treatment; for others, it can be dealt with in a supportive group. Depression is anger at something, turned in on the self. We must learn to deal with our anger and not suppress it.

8. Be decisive! Indecision can result in depending on others' opinions, advice, and affirmation. Practice being decisive by allowing yourself to make mistakes and not feeling like a failure. Mistakes are steps toward success. You are human. All humans make mistakes. Allow others to make mistakes. Do ask others for counsel; then make your own decisions and stand by them, good or bad. Decision making is a learning process. Don't copy others! What's good for them might not work for you.

9. Enhance your appearance to fit your own individual, unique style. Get into the best possible physical shape, exercise, and eat healthily. Assess your own needs for improving your hairstyle, wardrobe, and makeup.

10. Institute a policy of learning something new every day. This will enhance both your self-esteem and your intelligence. Knowledge is power! Reading is a great source of knowledge. Lifelong education will stimulate intelligence.

s u m m a r y

This letter to a friend by the Reverend Valerie J. Bridgeman Davis puts this book in perspective for me.

To Seleta

For all those times you sistered me
    you know,
       Laughed at not-too-funny jokes, sat for hours
talking about nothing in particular
and everything in general,
       cried when you knew I was burdened
       with cares you could not carry for me,
and were just there,
I thank you.

For all those times you mothered me:
　　you know,
　　Corrected me when I would be judgmental,
cared for me when I had neither the strength
nor desire to care for myself,
　　loved me when I proved unlovely
　　or unlovable,
and just accepted me.
I thank you.
For all those times you befriended me:
　　you know,
　　Urged me on to a new plane of thinking,
raised my sight and my vision when I insisted on looking down,
encouraged, strengthened, even protected my faith
in God when I would have given up,
I thank you.
　　You have been more to me than any one word could
describe:
　　And for all you have been to me
Thank you.

THE HEALING OF SISTERS

The women whose life stories you have shared in this book
have one thing in common. They dared to reach out to another woman who "sistered" them through a difficult period
in their lives. Often, the help we want is not the help we really need. And too often, the help we need requires us to be
vulnerable with information about ourselves that we would
rather keep safely inside. But God has provided us with a
wide and varied community of friends, associates, sisters, and
peers—all who hold within their very being the resources
that can help us through our journey of pain to wholeness.

In the United Methodist Church we have an agency that advocates for the full equality and participation of all women at every level of our church. It is called the Commission on the Status and Role of Women (COSROW). One of the founding members, the Rev. Nancy Grissom Self, taught us that there are five kinds of people that we need in our lives to assist us in growing toward our fullest potential. I now call them the Five Caring "C's." The five C's are people to comfort us, clarify issues with us, confront us, collaborate with us, and celebrate with us.

I have enclosed a chart for your use in determining where you can go to find the help you need in the days ahead as you continue your search for inner healing (see "A Personal Support Grid" in the appendix). What I found surprising as I first filled in this chart was that I had the names of my husband and my daughter in almost every area, yet I knew that my needs were not being met. I came to the startling conclusion that I was placing unrealistic expectations upon these two individuals, who do love me but cannot be everything I need. The real trick is to know what you need and when you need it, and then, who to go to for it. God has provided persons in both our personal and professional lives who can respond to every need. We must be so in touch with our inner selves that we can manipulate our environment in order to be made whole.

In my life, I looked to my spouse, Chuck, to be comforter, clarifier, collaborator, and lover at all times. He is a friend, but his personality does not permit him to be my comforter. He is more able to confront me in my pity party moods and not join in. This helps me to get angry enough that I move. Then, when I know that I need comfort, there are a couple of individuals who love me almost as much as my mother. They cannot see my faults and will stroke me and nurture me until I feel loved in spite of myself. If I need comfort, I used to call Jessica Ingram, but as our relationship grew and matured, she challenged and confronted me too! So, now I call Lucille Jackson or Deborah Tate or a "sweet" friend! All of these persons provide me with the "glue" that keeps me together.

In Galatians 6:2, we are exhorted to "bear one another's burdens." Burdens here refers to the temporary overburden that we might have, as opposed to the everyday load referred to in verse five of this chapter. In our times, when the pains of life are rising up to cause us undue stress, we need to be able to reach out and find someone with whom to share our situation. This sharing is not to provide quick-fix, single-solution answers. What we most often need are empathetic individuals who will weep with us, rejoice with us, and sit quietly listening and being a supportive presence. After sharing with a friend like this, we feel lighter, for someone has "heard." Someone has absorbed some of our pain and relieved some of our burden.

I thank God for the men friends, brothers, peers, and associates in my life. I have found, however, that when the cracks of the past begin to ache, strain, and pull at my guts, it's a sister, a woman who allows herself to "feel" with me that I want to talk to. When we are in pain, we need comfort and understanding. When we are hurting, advice is not the answer. Often times, just the ability to be held, to cry silently, and to hear the words, "It's all right," are the ingredients that push us toward tomorrow with hope.

After a major surgery, my husband was there, trying to share and to show tenderness. But medicine, his sitting with me, or the nurse's backrubs did not do the trick. It was only when my mother arrived and I was able to put my head on her breast and feel her heartbeat and have her hold me, without words, that I began to feel better.

THE STEPS TO WHOLENESS

Broken vessels are never made perfect, but they are perfectly made. The making process involves many diverse steps, none of which are identical, nor is any of these steps the end result. Terry, Zinnia, Belle, Briana, Shala, Carla, Linda, and you will have to repeat these seven steps over and over again as different broken pieces of our childhood begin to rise from our subconscious and demand our attention. With every cycle of submitting to the steps you will find many benefits.

- Your faith, trust, and confidence in both God and yourself will have grown because of the stretching of your mental and spiritual boundaries.

- You will find your world enlarged. God comforts us, but not simply to make us comfortable. God provides us with comfort in order to make us more aware of the pain in others and to give us an extra measure of sensitivity, which helps us to become more creative and more resourceful in making a difference in the world.

- You will view the world with a new perspective.

- Hope will replace helplessness in your world.

- Negativity will be lessened as the positive becomes more forceful in your life.

- Your self-esteem and self-confidence will be motivators to those whose lives you touch.

- It is not your words alone that make an impact on the world. It is your attitude that is contagious, life-changing, and radically powerful.

The most important aspect of undergoing the pain required to move through these seven steps is the ability to actually meet the woman who lives inside of your exterior shell. Most of us live with our surface self, that self we present to the world in order to protect ourselves. These seven steps move us inward, causing us to peel off the layers of pretend; to discard unwanted and unhealthy actions as we replace them with new, healthy, and growth-producing patterns of living. Every woman in this book has learned to agree with God. This is an essential principle of being a healthy Christian. For God is Love. God is Life. God is Light. God is Unlimited Potential.

As we walk through life recognizing our wounds, we recognize that God desires our wholeness and our health. As we admit our wounds, we come to realize that God knew our deepest secrets and loved us all the while. When we move to the point of sharing our pain with a significant other, we comprehend that God has always provided rams in the thickets" (Gen. 22:13) to spare our sacrificing our very selves. And when we finally confess on an emotional level with soul-cleansing crying and sobbing, we remember that it is God's bowels of compassion that grieved over us so much that Jesus was sent to save us. The decision to attempt reconciliation causes us to remember and to reflect upon the passion and suffering of Jesus Christ, who willingly gave his life in order to bring us back into at-one-ment with the same God who used to commune daily with humankind.

Choosing to be different is our salvation. It is our choice. We can move to this point and make the choice: "The pain I have undergone is enough. I will not accept repeating this pain." Or we can remain stuck in our brokenness. The choice to be different brings new life and makes us new creations. This decision must be made on a daily basis. Old habits have a way of sneaking back into our lives if we are not conscious and consistent in our commitment to choose new life everyday.

If you have not come to appreciate the fact that these seven steps—recognition, admission, sharing, confession, reconciliation, choosing to be different, and choosing daily—are the identical steps that we take for receiving new life in Jesus Christ, I invite you to reflect upon this now. I must recognize that I am a sinner in need of God's grace. I must admit to myself that I am not God and need a higher power to take charge of my life. Then I must confess with my mouth that Jesus Christ is Lord of all to the glory of God, which is usually done in a public place as we share with significant others. The work of the church is to recognize that we are all hungry beggars seeking for the Bread of Life, and when we find it, we invite others to the feast. Then I must accept reconciliation and justification with God, which is mine through the work of Jesus at Calvary. Because I am so grateful for this free gift of grace, I choose to offer what I am, who I am, and what I have to this Christ. This initial choice to be different is a one-time affair. God will never leave me or forsake me. God does give me the gift of choice, and daily I must decide if I am going to follow the way to eternal life, which is lived one day at a time. The gift of the Holy Spirit is given to me, as a friend, a confidant, a listener, a guide, and a comforter who will lead me day by day to my truth.

THE REST OF THE STORY

In the years since the first writing, much has occurred in the life of these sisters who have touched your life. Terry has been ordained, has changed denominations, and now pastors a local congregation called "New Life."

Zinnia's divorce is final and she is working to make a life for herself and her son.

In a beautiful, candlelit ceremony, on the fifteenth day of December, Belle walked down the aisle to become the bride she always dreamed of. She asked her pastor, her dad, and myself to be a part of the wedding service. I cannot describe the awe I experienced watching my sister in a beautiful white dress become a bride indeed. She has moved to another state, graduated from seminary, and is busy being happy as wife and pastor.

Briana has also been ordained, completed seminary, and works in a local, affirming congregation where she is in charge of the ministry to women.

Shala has received two promotions, bought a home, alone, and gave a huge party to celebrate her birthday and new self-identity! She continues to work at her relationship with her dad. Her grandparents have since died.

Carla retired as a pastor. She continued to call us together for retreats, even as she ministered to her own soul, until her death.

I have written more, preached more, retreated and advanced more as I continue to struggle to fulfill my potential in God. My love affair with Chuck continues as we work at our marriage and take time for each other on a weekly basis. My work in the community continues to refresh and renew me. I continue to feel the cracks and strains, and look for new glue to keep the broken places of my life together. But I know my worth in the kingdom, and I affirm my gifts, my graces. I also affirm my weaknesses and places where I need to grow. I like the Linda who is evolving and praise our God for using me!

As I began this summary with a poem, I will close with a familiar song which speaks to my brokenness and my personal relationship with God. It is "The Broken Vessel" by Andrae Crouch.

The Potter saw a vessel
That was broken by the wind and rain;
And He sought with so much compassion
to make it over again.

Oh! I was that vessel
that no one thought was good.
I cried, "Lord, You're the Potter
and I am the clay, make me over again, today."

Then God picked up all the pieces
of my broken life that day.
Then He made me a new vessel
and revived my soul again.

Thanks be to God for the unspeakable gifts of women who have shared my pain and shared their pain with me. God has made us "vessels of honor"—those who are willing and determined that all broken vessels have the opportunity to be made whole!

appendix

A PERSONAL SUPPORT GRID

	Role	Personal Life	Professional Life
COMFORTER			
CLARIFIER			
CONFRONTER			
COLLABORATOR			
CELEBRATOR			

Fill in the names of persons who provide these functions of support for you. Some may be near, some may be far, some may be authors, heroes, or heroines. When you feel the need for support, to whom and or to what do you turn? You can manipulate your environment. Some aspects of these roles might include:

Comforter: The one who listens and reassures you that you are okay, significant, worthy, lovable, and accepted, without hesitation, reservation, or qualifications.

Clarifier: The one who listens, takes you seriously, reflects, suggests options, assists you in focusing what the issues are and what your next response and or steps might be.

Confronter: The one who nudges, urges, pushes you to take yourself by the nape of the neck and get on with dealing with your issues and challenges you to be in charge of your life and gives you honest feedback that can assist you to see with proper perspective.

Collaborator: The one who pitches in to help you to overcome the inertia in yourself and can move with you into the scary tasks and tedious detail work to help you to accomplish goals. This one is there to be supportive in more ways than words of encouragement.

Celebrator: The one to whom you can "wow" about your triumphs and successes, not withholding yourself. This one can joyfully applaud you and celebrate these events with you.

∽∾

What is critical to this exercise is the recognition that persons can take initiative to create an adequate support system in both the personal and public arenas of their lives. I hope that you will be able to realize that no one person, regardless of who they are, can "do it all" for you.

A Self-Test on Self-Esteem for Women

Research on self-esteem in women has shown that women with low self-esteem are emotionally repressed, not satisfied with their body images, uncertain of their futures, afraid of success, and have many self-negating and self-doubting behaviors. This exercise is intended to help you identify whether or not low self-esteem has hampered or restricted you or caused pain in your life planning.

Women who have feelings of low self-esteem tend to judge themselves and others without mercy. They try to cover up by being perfectionists, controlling, contemptuous, gossipy, or trying to take care of too many.

1. In what ways do you attempt to cover your feelings of inadequacy?

_____

_____

Women who have low self-esteem tend to isolate themselves and to feel uneasy around persons whom they do not know, especially authority figures.

2. When did you last try to "hide" in a group of people?

_____

_____

3. Do you have difficulty dealing with persons in authority? What generally happens in your relationships with authority figures?

_____

_____

Women with low self-esteem tend to be approval seekers and will do almost anything to get people to like them. They are extremely loyal—even in the face of evidence that indicates loyalty is undeserved.

4. In what ways do you seek approval from family and friends?

_____

_____

5. In what relationship do you need to question your undeserved loyalty?

_____

_____

Women with low self-esteem tend to be intimidated by angry people and by personal criticism, causing them to feel anxious.

6. When have you recently felt intimidated by an angry person?

_____

_____

7. How do you respond to personal criticism?

_____

_____

Women with low self-esteem tend to be either super responsible or super irresponsible. We try to solve others' problems or expect others to solve ours. This keeps us from looking at and working on our own behavior.

8. Name areas of your life in which you feel either super responsible or super irresponsible.

_____

_____

Women with low self-esteem feel guilty when they stand up for themselves or act assertively. They give in to others instead of taking care of themselves.

9. Identify a recent situation in which you were afraid to express your feelings and gave in to others.

_____

_____

Women with low self-esteem deny, minimize, or repress feelings from their traumatic childhoods. They lose the ability to express their feelings and are unaware of the impact this has on their lives.

10. How do you express your feelings when something upsets you at work or in relationships?

_____

_____

Women with low self-esteem are primarily dependent personalities who are terrified of rejection or abandonment. They tend to stay in jobs or relationships that are harmful to them. Their fears can either stop them from ending hurtful relationships or prevent them from entering into healthy, rewarding ones.

11. In which of your relationships (with spouse, child, or friend) do you fear rejection or abandonment?

_____

_____

12. How do you deal with this fear?

_____

_____

Women with low self-esteem have difficulty with intimate relationships. They are insecure and lack trust in others. Their boundaries aren't clearly defined, and they become too emotionally enmeshed with the needs of their spouses, children, and friends.

13. Describe the difficulties you are having with an intimate relationship.

_____

_____

_____

Women with low self-esteem have a strong need to be in control. They overreact to changes over which they have no control.

14. What do you fear most when change occurs and you are not in control?

_____

_____

_____

Women with low self-esteem have difficulty finishing projects.

15. What was the last project you did not complete or procrastinated on?

_____

_____

_____

Affirmations for Women

Affirmations replace the negative statements that we too often make to ourselves and about ourselves. Our mind cannot hold or process two thoughts at the same time. This list of positive affirmations can program out your negative, self-critical thoughts. Have you ever heard yourself say, "I'll never get this right" or "I'm so dumb"? These statements have been programmed into your subconscious mind. You can change. You can repeat these affirmations to yourself while driving, walking, sitting, or even working. Whenever or wherever you find yourself being self-critical, begin to affirm who you are—a wonderful, unique individual.

Twice daily, stand facing a mirror. Look yourself directly in the eye, and say aloud, "(Your name), I love you and accept you exactly as you are. There is hope for you. You are worthwhile. God has good just for you, and you walk in blessings!"

Other affirmations that are short and easy to remember are listed below for you. Use them in the time you spend driving, exercising, waiting in checkout lines, or while sitting in solitude.

I AM FREE OF PAIN, WORRY, AND FEAR.

I ENJOY PERFECT PEACE AND WELL-BEING.

In every aspect of my life, I am guided to my highest potential and greatest fulfillment.

I have the gift of serenity. Problems and struggles fade in the peace of God.

The perfect solution to every problem will manifest in time. I wait in a state of blessedness.

All things are possible for me to achieve through God's love.

God's divine love works to heal me and strengthen me now. God loves me.

God has provided for me.

God is at work for me, in me, and through me, calming me and guiding me to still waters.

I release the pain of the past and welcome the good that is mine to claim.

Stay away from demanding, specific, time-oriented affirmations. Simply affirm yourself, your life, your worth, and your wonderful future. When you make affirmations, you are programming your unconscious to become willing to let go of the old patterns and tapes and to move into new, healthy, joyous, and blessed ways of living and attracting God's good.

I'm Crying Through

I'm crying through the pain,
the sunshine—the rain,
silence and defeat,
those who've left me under their feet.

I'm crying through rejection,
the heartaches and heartbreaks,
the inexplicable shame,
the scornings of my name.

I'm crying through persecution,
those things that I've been told,
for if I endure the fire,
I'll come forth as pure gold.

I'm crying through ignorance,
prejudices, myths, and hurts,
the "you'll never amount to anything,"
and those who've treated me like dirt.

I'm crying through my fears,
of "I'm never going to make it,"
of "Lord, I just can't take it,"
of "fake it 'til you make it."

I'm crying through the lies,
those I've even chosen to buy,
those words that got me high,
those which left me standing by.

I'm crying through disappointment,
anger, rage, and feelings bent,
revenge is never sweet,
Only God's love will defeat.

I'm crying through my battles,
chains that had me shackled,
Still holding my head up high,
after the pointing fingers and cackles.

I'm crying through the through,
On the other side, I'm renewed,
That which I thought had me bound,
In it, it was me I found.

—Phanessa A. Gray

I've Been Mixed Like Cornbread

I've been mixed like cornbread
And I'm not that instant brand.
Measured out, not by metered cup
But with the skill of a Knowing hand.

The flour of my soul and
The meal of my mind
Rises with the yeast and
The salts of time.
I've been mixed like cornbread.

Two eggs for self-identity
A dash of sugar to make me sweet
Add the day-old fatback drippings
And this cornbread is complete.
I've been mixed like cornbread.

I tickle your tastebuds to a salivary greeting
After exactly 23 minutes at 375°
Top me off with real fresh butter
You welcome our meeting as I now arrive.
I've been mixed like cornbread.

So—serve me up I'm a favorite dish
With the likes of collard greens, buttermilk or fish
I've been mixed like cornbread
And I'm here to compliment
Your first course in life!

—Raedorah C. Stewart ©1988

bibliography

Ahlers, Julia, ed. *Women's Psalms*. Minneapolis: St. Mary's Press, 1992.

Angelou, Maya. *I Know Why the Caged Bird Sings*. New York: Bantam Books, 1970.

Avery, Bylyle. *An Altar of Words: Wisdom, Comfort, and Inspiration for African American Women*. New York: Broadway Books, 1998.

Bankston, Marjory. *Braided Streams*. San Diego: Lura Media Press, 1985.

Bibbs, Stephanie. *Women's Liberation: Jesus Style*. Lansing, Mich.: Ruarch Communications, 1998.

Borysenko, Joan. *A Woman's Journey to God*. New York: Riverhead Books, 1999.

Breathnach, Sarah Ban. *Simple Abundance: A Daybook of Comfort and Joy*. New York : Warner Books, 1995.

Casey, Karen. *Change Your Mind and Your Life Will Follow*. Boston: Conari Press, 2005.

Cornish, Grace. *Ten Bad Choices That Ruin Black Women's Lives*. New York: Crown Publishing Group, 1999.

Douglas, Kelly Brow. *Sexuality and the Black Church*. Maryknoll, N.Y.: Orbis Books, 1999.

Edelman, Marian Wright. *Guide My Feet*. Boston: Beacon Press, 1995.

Ellison, Sheila, ed. *If Women Ruled the World*. San Francisco: Inner Ocean Publishing, 2004.

Essex, Barbara. *Bad Girls of the Bible: Exploring Women of Questionable Virtue*. Cleveland: Pilgrim Press, 1999.)

Fortune, Marie. *Sexual Violence: The Sin Revisited*. Cleveland: Pilgrim Press, 2005.

Hollies, Linda H. *Taking Back My Yesterdays: Lessons in Forgiving and Moving Forward with Your Life*. Cleveland: Pilgrim Press, 1997.

———. *Jesus and Those Bodacious Women: Life Lessons from One Sister to Another*. Cleveland: Pilgrim Press, 1998.

———. *Mother Goose Meets a Woman Called Wisdom: A Short Course in the Art of Self-Determination*. Cleveland: Pilgrim Press, 1999.

———. *On Their Way to Wonderful: A Journey with Ruth and Naomi*. Cleveland: Pilgrim Press, 2004.

———. *Bodacious Womanist Wisdom*. (Cleveland: Pilgrim Press, 2005.

———. *Living Bountifully!: The Blessing of Responsible Stewardship*. Cleveland: Pilgrim Press, 2005.

hooks, bell. *Feminist Theory*. Cambridge, Mass.: South End Press, 2000.

Kidd, Sue Monk. *The Dance of the Dissident Daughter*. San Francisco: HarperCollins, 2002.

Miller, Jean Baker. *Towards a New Psychology of Women*. Boston: Beacon Press, 1976.

Nelson, Jill. *Straight: No Chaser*. New York: G.P. Putnam, 1997.

Poling, Nancy Werking. *Victim to Survivor: Women Recovering from Clergy Sexual Abuse*. Cleveland: Pilgrim Press, 1999.

Rice, Patty. *Reinventing the Women*. New York: Penguin Group, 2003.

Richardson, Brenda and Wade. *What Mama Couldn't Tell Us about Love*. New York: HarperCollins, 1999.

Robinson, Lori. *I Will Survive*. New York: Seal Press, 2002.

Sark. *The Bodacious Book of Succulence*. New York: Simon and Shuster, 1998.

Seamands, David. *The Healing of Memories*. Wheaton, Ill.: Victor Books, 1985.

Taylor, Susan. *Lessons in Living*. New York: Anchor Books, 1995.

Townes, Emilie M. *Embracing the Spirit*. Maryknoll, N.Y.: Orbis Books, 1997.

Trible, Phyllis. *Texts of Terror*. Philadelphia: Fortress Press, 1984.

Viorst, Judith. *Necessary Losses*. New York: Fawcett Gold Medal, 1986.

Weems, Renita. *Just a Sister Away*. San Diego: Lura Media Press, 1998.

_____. *Showing Mary*. West Bloomfield: Walk Worthy Press, 2002.

White, Evelyn. *The Black Women's Health Book*. Seattle: Seal Press, 1990.

Wimberly, Anne Streaty. *Soul Stories: African American Christian Education*. Nashville: Abingdon Press, 1994.

Wuellner, Flora Slosson. *Prayer, Stress, and Our Inner Wounds*. Nashville: Upper Room Press, 1985.

Wyatt, Gail Elizabeth. *Stolen Women*. New York: John Wiley and Sons, 1997.

Vanzant, Iyanla. *Until Today!: Daily Devotions for Spiritual Growth and Peace of Mind*. New York : Simon & Schuster, 2000.

Other books from The Pilgrim Press

LIVING BOUNTIFULLY
The Blessings of Responsible Stewardship

LINDA H. HOLLIES

0-8298-1676-3/paper/128 pages/$16.00

Jesus spent a great deal of time speaking to his followers about money and property. Hollies feels that—like Jesus—this is an issue which women in general and women of color in particular, need to talk about and address in their personal lives. In *Living Bountifully*, Hollies shares her lessons, strategies, and experiences of godly stewardship.

ON THEIR WAY TO WONDERFUL
A Journey with Ruth and Naomi

LINDA H. HOLLIES

0-8298-1604-6/paper/130 pages/$18.00

This resource is an exploration of multicultural marriage (Ruth and Boaz) as well as diversity and racism in Scripture (Ruth, a Moabite who God allows to enter the forbidden Jewish bloodline). Women will relate to this book as it touches on issues that impact their lives, such as making critical decisions, handling relationships, and renewal of self and soul.

To order these or any other books from The Pilgrim Press call or write to:

THE PILGRIM PRESS
700 PROSPECT AVENUE EAST
CLEVELAND, OHIO 44115-1100

Phone orders: 1-800-537-3394 · FAX ORDERS: 216-736-2206

Please include shipping charges of $5.00 for the first book and 75¢ for each additional book. Or order from our web sites at www.thepilgrimpress.com and www.ucpress.com.

Prices subject to change without notice.